Graham Handley MA

Brodie's Notes on Charles Dickens's

Our Mutual Friend

Pan Books London and Sydney

First published 1979 by Pan Books Ltd
Cavaye Place, London SW10 9PG
3 4 5 6 7 8 9

ISBN 0 330 50149 6
Filmset in Great Britain by
Northumberland Press Ltd, Gateshead, Tyne and Wear
Printed and bound by
Richard Clay (The Chaucer Press) Ltd, Bungay, Suffolk

Contents

Page references in these Notes are to the Penguin edition of *Our Mutual Friend*, but as references are also given to particular Books and chapters, the Notes may be used with any edition of the novel.

To the student

A close reading of the set book is the student's primary task. These Notes will help to increase your understanding and appreciation of the book, and to stimulate *your own* thinking about it; *they are in no way intended as a substitute* for a thorough knowledge of the book.

The author and his work

The biographies and critical studies of Charles Dickens – and they show no sign of abating – are testimony to the powerful hold he has exerted on the reading public ever since the first appearance of *Sketches by Boz* (1833–4). In the eyes of many he stands next to Shakespeare; television plays and scripts are written about his life, or aspects of it, and his books are filmed, adapted, or turned into musicals (Lionel Bart's *Oliver*, for example) with flattering regularity. The biography of his friend and adviser John Forster (*Charles Dickens*) tantalizes both by what it reveals and what it omits, while F. R. Leavis, perhaps the most influential critic of the novel in the twentieth century, has recanted his view (expressed in *The Great Tradition*, 1948) that Dickens was merely 'a great entertainer'. This Study Aid can do no more than give the outlines of a crowded literary life, at the back of which lies an equally crowded social and emotional one. The experiences of a great writer are shared with his readers, but Dickens invites – indeed demands – imaginative reading; an awareness of his time; a sense of historical (and, especially, social) perspective. A select reading list is included at the end of this section to guide students to a wider knowledge of his life, his writing, and the critical appraisal his work has received.

Born in 1812 in Portsmouth, the second-eldest son in a family of eight, Dickens was to see his improvident father and the rest of the family incarcerated in the Marshalsea Debtors' Prison in London. This experience received full treatment in *Little Dorrit* (1855–7); at the time, Charles spent six weeks in Warren's blacking warehouse before his father's release and his own despatch to school. Again he was haunted by what he had endured, and part of the autobiographical element of *David Copperfield* records the anguish of that experience.

Dickens lived as he wrote, with zest and with an unrivalled capacity for giving himself up to both ecstasy and melancholy – later incorporating either or both into his fiction. He worked for a time in an attorney's office, then as a reporter in Doctors' Commons, while teaching himself shorthand and quickly striking out as a writer under the pseudonym of 'Boz'.

The first sketches referred to above were followed by the episodic *Pickwick Papers* (1836–7), originally commissioned as a vehicle for the artist Seymour. Their verve and humour, their presentation of a range of eccentric and idiosyncratic characters, and the animated and ebullient style and control of situation they showed, established the young author who, even before he had completed the Pickwickian marathon, found himself editor of *Bentley's Miscellany*. He also began to write *Oliver Twist*, the first number of which appeared in the magazine in February 1837. But in May his beloved sister-in-law Mary Hogarth died; she had lived with her sister and Charles since their marriage, and Dickens adored her. She died in his arms, and he took a ring from her finger and wore it until his own death. He dreamed of her continually, and there is little doubt that the heroines of Dickens's fiction are derived from the purity and perfection he found in Mary Hogarth.

Oliver Twist was followed by *Nicholas Nickleby* (1838–9), an attack on the Yorkshire farm schools. Dickens was always a prolific writer, and *The Old Curiosity Shop* (1840), *Barnaby Rudge* (1841) and *Martin Chuzzlewit* (1843–4) indicate his capacity for hard work and dedication to the career he had already successfully established. Active socially, theatrically, politically, philanthropically (glance at his letters to see the amazing range of his interests and concerns), there were now longer gaps than hitherto between his novels. But increasingly he evinced a growing sense of artistic structure: from *Dombey and Son* (1846–8) onwards, that awareness is present in the complex handling of plot and sub-plot, of contrast and parallel, of image and symbol. Of course this leads to the creation of the long and bulky novel, and the length sometimes acts as a deterrent, for modern readers, to total immersion in Dickens.

These great novels occupy the middle section of Dickens's writing career, with *David Copperfield* (1848–50) perhaps the best loved, and *Bleak House* (1852–3) the most aesthetically pleasing. Between that and the prison-filled *Little Dorrit* (1855–7) Dickens sandwiched a small masterpiece, *Hard Times* (1854), set in the (for him) distant provincial location of Preston (Coketown). He had spent much of his time in Paris, and a reading of Carlyle's *French Revolution* is said to have inspired *A Tale of Two Cities* (1859) with its graphic reconstruction of events great and small in that turbulent era.

Strictly speaking the final period of Dickens's writing begins with *Great Expectations* (1860–61), which is thought by some critics to be the high-water-mark of his achievement. It is rich in atmosphere and in the experiences of childhood, and, as in *Our Mutual Friend* (1864–5), there is no evidence of any falling off in either the verve or the vivacity of the writing, or in the imagination that informed it. The final work, *Edwin Drood* (1870), which seemed to be breaking new ground, was left incomplete by the author's death.

Like most great writers, Dickens is surrounded by anecdote and gossip, by the interpretations of the sensational and the investigations of the peripheral. The student of *Our Mutual Friend*, or of any of the stories or novels for that matter, should concentrate on Dickens's works. Dickens was, perhaps still is – despite our turning away to media other than print – a national institution: the great fireside communicator of his own time and well into this century. But for many of us the fireside has gone; and the voices that speak to us are not rich in humanity or in social, moral or spiritual concern. Dickens's voice speaks for all of these: that is why we should read him so attentively today. For as we see Oliver in *Oliver Twist* ask for more; Dombey of *Dombey and Son* awaken to love for his daughter after years of silent rejection; Pip in *Great Expectations* discover himself through his affection for Magwitch; and, in *Our Mutual Friend* Lizzie Hexam sacrifice so much for her brother Charley's education, we touch those aspects of human love beside which the computers and screens of our own time are ephemeral and irrelevant.

Further reading

The Dickens Encyclopaedia, Ed. Hayward (Routledge)

The Dickens Theatre, Robert Garis (Oxford University Press)

Dickens the Novelist, Sylvère Monod (University of Oklahoma Press)

A Reader's Guide to Charles Dickens, Philip Hobsbaum (Thames and Hudson)

Background and Foreground

When Dickens began to write *Our Mutual Friend* he was fifty-two years old and travelling incessantly on his reading tours; he was also emotionally involved with the actress Ellen Ternan. As early as 1861, after he had completed *Great Expectations*, he had decided upon *Our Mutual Friend* for the title of his next novel; he managed before the serial began in May 1864 (it continued until November 1865) to be well ahead with the actual writing of the monthly numbers, something he had not always achieved in the past. The theme was to be the effects of the corruption of money, as seen through the various strands in society, and the mounds of dust are therefore the central symbol – and indeed the central fact – of the novel. At that time, and earlier, great heaps of refuse could provide a rich income for the contractor who carted them away and sifted through them, not merely for valuables but for matter which could be sold for melting down or pulping. Among the ingredients of the mounds there were, for example, ashes that could be used in the production of bricks; there was plenty of soot for the vegetable plot; bones for the manufacturers of soap; and rags for paper-making. In the 1820s one dust heap fetched between £4,000 and £5,000.

Also of profound interest to Dickens (and used in this novel) were, for example, the longshoremen and their 'ghastly trade', which provided him with Gaffer Hexam, Rogue Riderhood and – the rebel against such a life – Lizzie. Dickens did not begin the novel until the autumn of 1863, and by the following February he had written sufficient material for four numbers. It was at that point that his illustrator Marcus Stone provided him with the noteworthy eccentric who was to play a part in the working out of the plot. It was in the St Giles district of London that he found the original of Mr

Venus, 'preserver of animals and birds, and articulator of human bones'. Dickens actually introduced him into the last chapter of the second number (each of the numbers had either three or four chapters, with the exception of the last, which was a double number containing five chapters).

His personal pressures were heavy, and he observed, 'I have grown hard to satisfy, and write very slowly. And I have so much – not fiction – that *will* be thought of when I don't want to think of it, that I am forced to take more care than I once took.' The first number achieved a sale of 30,000, but there was a drop of 5,000 for the second before that figure was eventually reached again. By 29 July he was beset by illness, and had fallen behind with the novel; he rallied sufficiently to meet the writing load of the autumn, but by February 1865 he was incapacitated again, and could take no exercise. The next two months were agony, and he went abroad to try to obtain the peace and quiet he needed for the book. Returning from France on 9 June 1865 he suffered the terrible shock of being involved in a serious railway accident. Forster quotes Dickens's words as follows:

> I . . . worked for hours among the dying and dead. I was in the carriage that did not go over, but went off the line, and hung over the bridge in an inexplicable manner. No words can describe the scene.

This was written on the day after the accident that was to haunt him for the rest of his life; with an irony worthy of his own fictional making, he died on 9 June five years later. As he was to write in the Postscript to *Our Mutual Friend*, 'Mr and Mrs Boffin (in their manuscript dress of receiving Mr and Mrs Lammle at breakfast) were on the South-Eastern Railway with me, in a terribly destructive accident . . . I remember with devout thankfulness that I can never be much nearer parting company with my readers for ever, than I was then, until there shall be written against my life, the two words with which I have this day closed this book – THE END.'

In an interesting article in the magazine *Nineteenth Century Fiction* (December 1965), Harland Nelson suggests that Dickens was somewhat indebted to Henry Mayhew's classic study *London Labour and the London Poor*, both for the kind of old woman portrayed in Betty Higden and for the close look at Gaffer Hexam, the river scavenger, early in the novel. He points out that in Mayhew's account the description of the dredgerman occurs some four pages after the account of Betty Higden. Mayhew's method was to investigate the various occupations and interview an individual in some depth, taking down as completely as possible everything that was said to him. By a curious coincidence, the final version of Mayhew's work was printed in 1864–5, just at the time when Dickens was writing *Our Mutual Friend*, but the interested student is advised to follow up the article referred to above and test his own judgement in order to see whether or not Dickens used one of the great social documents of his own time, indeed of any time. As London background to Dickens Mayhew is invaluable, and the reader is referred to the four-volume edition of his works published by Dover Books, and *The Unknown Mayhew*, ed. E. P. Thompson and Eileen Yeo (Pelican Classics).

The Foreground referred to in the heading to this section is the physical locale of the main areas of the action. These are listed below in alphabetical order for each identification, but again the student who is interested in Dickens's London is advised to make his own 'map' of the area with the Dickensian locations marked on it. No attempt has been made here to go much beyond the confines of London; though Lizzie, we are told, works in a paper-mill in Oxfordshire, and Betty Higden's journey certainly ends there.

The Albany (Nowadays called simply 'Albany'); a large building on the north side of Piccadilly in the West End, between Sackville Street and Burlington House. Fledgeby lived in chambers in Albany, despite his meanness. It was the resort of men of fashion throughout the nineteenth century.

Bank of England Sometimes referred to as 'The Old Lady of Threadneedle Street', since its main frontage is to Threadneedle Street in the City of London in the area known as The Bank. Bella feels that she would like a bright copper shovel so that she could do an hour's 'gardening' there.

Battle Bridge Prior to 1830 this was the name for King's Cross. This is associated with the Mounds. Mr Boffin lived over Maiden Lane way, which is now York Road, in the direction of Holloway. The dust and refuse heaps were certainly real, some being to the south of King's Cross Station just where the Gray's Inn Road begins.

Bethnal Green At the time, Bethnal Green was a large and heavily populated village on the eastern outskirts of London proper. Eugene and Mortimer lure Bradley Headstone into following them into this dangerous area.

Blackheath Then a pleasant village close to the River Thames, lying to the south of Greenwich; this is where John and Bella take a 'modest little cottage' after their marriage.

Brentford On the north bank of the Thames beyond Kew Bridge. Now a built-up London suburb with many factories and industrial buildings, there is little to show that this was once a favourite riverside resort of Londoners. Betty Higden lived in one of the 'back settlements'. Into these Bella and Mrs Boffin and Rokesmith went to find her, going on foot from The Three Magpies.

Cavendish Square In the fashionable West End close to Oxford Circus, where Wegg had a corner stall for some years, and where the Boffins had their mansion after Wegg took over at the Bower.

Chancery Lane Near the Law Courts, where John Rokesmith first saw Mr Boffin.

Charing Cross Hungerford Market stood where the station now is, but it was demolished in 1862. When Eugene was at Charing Cross he saw Dolls staggering about there.

Chelsea Large and populous village then, and a favourite resort of Londoners, Wegg referring to his ferryman father there on one occasion.
Children's Hospital i.e. in Great Ormond Street, the hospital to which little Johnny is taken and where he dies, with his toys and his memory of the 'boofer lady'.
Chiswick On the north bank of the Thames to the east of Brentford; it was as far as Hexam went on his scavenging.
Church Street, Smith Square Very close to the Houses of Parliament, where Jenny lived with the drunken Dolls. Church Street is now known as Dean Stanley Street.
Clerkenwell The area lying to the south of Islington in which Mr Venus carried on his business which was not approved by Pleasant Riderhood though she later overcame her aversion and married him.
Clifford's Inn The oldest of the inns of Chancery; Rokesmith talks to Boffin about being his secretary in this place.
Covent Garden Market Now removed, but for many years the famous market very close to the Opera House, much beloved of Dickens. Dolls collapsed here after the street-arabs had set upon him.
Doctors' Commons A college of lawyers founded in 1768 with headquarters near St Paul's Cathedral. Its members had sole rights of practising in certain courts, Probate being one; Boffin tells Lightwood about his own experiences there, but gets the name wrong ('Doctor Scommons'). The College was dissolved in 1857.
Duke Street On the south side of Piccadilly, in the Jermyn Street area; the home of Twemlow.
Exchequer Coffee House Originally 'Oliver's', it was next-door to Westminster Hall. 'Julius Handford's' address was here.
Fenchurch Street In the city between Gracechurch Street and Aldgate; Bella waited on the corner of Fenchurch Street and Mincing Lane for the Cherub and caused quite some comment.

Fleet Street At the western end stood Temple Bar, removed in 1878; at the eastern end, with many newspaper offices, Fleet Street extends down to Ludgate Circus. It is constantly referred to in Dickens's books. Rokesmith followed Mr Boffin down Fleet Street after Boffin had been to see Mortimer Lightwood.

Goldsmith's Buildings Part of the Temple, where Mortimer Lightwood had his office.

Greenwich A favourite retreat of Londoners at the time; Bella goes down the river on a trip with her father, and later marries 'Rokesmith' at Greenwich Church.

Holloway The home of the R. Wilfer family. Still reasonably rural at the time of *Our Mutual Friend*, though its approach from Battle Bridge (King's Cross) was disfigured by dust heaps and waste lands.

Inner Temple Gate i.e. through which Dolls was assisted by Eugene Wrayburn.

Leadenhall Street In the City close to Fenchurch Street. It is suggested that it was in nearby Cornhill in the churchyard of St Peter's that Bradley made his impassioned appeal to Lizzie Hexam.

Limehouse The district on the north bank of the Thames east of Stepney in the area of the Commercial Road and the West India Dock Road. There we find the Six Jolly Fellowship Porters; the Hexams and Rogue Riderhood live in Limehouse Hole, and John Harmon tells us in soliloquy the true story of his past.

London Bridge Opened in 1831, Gaffer Hexam was between it and Southwark Bridge in the first scene of the novel.

Maiden Lane York Road, King's Cross. (See note on *Battle Bridge*.)

Millbank The road by the Thames extending from Vauxhall Bridge nearly to the Houses of Parliament. Jenny lived close by in Church Stret off Smith Square.

Mincing Lane A road leading off Fenchurch Street, where R.

Wilfer worked for Chicksey, Veneering and Stobbles.
Monument i.e. the landmark in Fish Street Hill/Monument Street, erected to commemorate the Great Fire of London and close to the spot where it commenced.
Old Kent Road i.e. the main road to Greenwich and Kent.
Old Palace Yard Adjoining the Houses of Parliament.
Piccadilly Fashionable West End Centre – of wealth and vice in the nineteenth century, as today.
Portman Square Fashionable area of the West End north of Oxford Street; in or near it lived Podsnap.
Ratcliffe Dockside district forming a large hamlet – even then regarded as being a very tough area.
Richmond Pleasant area, now a suburban town, on the Thames in Surrey.
Sackville Street A fashionable street off Piccadilly; the home of Alfred Lammle prior to his marriage.
St James's Church In Piccadilly, where the Lammles were married.
St James's Square South of Piccadilly; a haunt of Twemlow's.
St John's Church In Smith Square; near Jenny, and described by her as being 'hideous'. After suffering severe war damage the building was restored and is now used as a concert hall.
St Mary Axe A street in the City running into Leadenhall Street. The home, or front, of Pubsey and Co.
Six Jolly Fellowship Porters See note on *Limehouse*. The description of this public house suggests that it was based on 'The Grapes' in Narrow Street, Limehouse.
Smith Square See note on *Church Street*.
Southwark Bridge Its old name was Iron Bridge; Hexam is between this bridge and London Bridge in the first scene.
Stepney Green On the south side of the Mile End Road, it is considered by Silas Wegg to be 'remote'.
Strand Extends from Charing Cross to the Law Courts. Frequently mentioned by Dickens, and in his time he would have

seen its widening, the building of Charing Cross Station and the making of Trafalgar Square.

The Temple Between Fleet Street and the Embankment, and the centre of legal learning and study in England; where Mortimer Lightwood had his office.

Temple Bar Built in 1670–2 to mark the western boundary of the City but removed in 1878 and erected as the entrance to Theobald's Park in 1888.

Thames Street It runs alongside the north bank of the Thames, and is divided into Upper and Lower Thames Street, commencing from Blackfriars and ending just before The Tower.

The Tower The Tower of London alongside the Thames at the end of Lower Thames Street; Bella waited for her father on one occasion opposite Trinity House, which is nearby.

Vauxhall Bridge The first bridge was opened in 1816, and it is while they are crossing this bridge that Bradley and Charley see Eugene Wrayburn.

Waterloo Station i.e. the original, built in 1846, with just two platforms. Frank Milvey, Mrs Milvey, and Bella set off from there to witness the bedside marriage of Lizzie and Eugene Wrayburn.

Westminster Abbey The great Church of England abbey, opposite the Houses of Parliament, where English monarchs are crowned. Dickens is buried there, close to Chaucer, Shakespeare and Dryden. 'Abbey' Potterson was thought by some to be called after Westminster Abbey.

Westminster Hall At the north-west angle of it stood the coffee house that was given as the address of Julius Handford.

Whitefriars Close to the Temple.

Whitehall Extending south from Trafalgar Square in the direction of the Houses of Parliament with many Government office buildings. At the time, the Metropolitan Police Office was at 4 Whitehall Buildings and it seems likely that it was here that John Harmon saw the placard announcing his own death in suspicious circumstances.

Plot

Even by Dickensian standards, the plot of *Our Mutual Friend* is complex, and it is made even more difficult to unravel by the narrative method, which switches from area to area, as will be seen from a chronological reading of the chapter summaries and the Notes that follow them. At the centre of the web is John Harmon, who is to inherit the Harmon estate – according to the will of his dust-contractor father – provided he marries Bella Wilfer. On his way home from abroad he is drugged and supposedly murdered; in fact he recovers, keeps hidden for a time, sheltered by the fact that the body of one of his assailants is mistaken for his. Then he reappears, assumes the name of Rokesmith, and lodges with the Wilfer family; he is thus giving himself the opportunity of observing Bella at close quarters. He makes himself known to the Boffins in his disguised identity, but they recognize him from the past: when he was a child they had been kind to him, and now they enter into a plot with him to keep his identity concealed, though their complicity is not easily understood by the reader.

The Boffins have, of course, inherited the Harmon money, but Mr Boffin has got himself involved with the unscrupulous Silas Wegg, who uncovers another Harmon will (which he believes will disinherit Boffin). Wegg plots with Venus to blackmail Boffin, but Venus reveals this intrigue to Boffin, and Wegg is finally discredited. The Boffins meanwhile have taken Bella as their companion, and Rokesmith proposes to her (in his false identity of course). In order to test Bella, Boffin affects to be miserly (Bella having earlier been determined to marry money). Ultimately all is revealed, for Mortimer Lightwood recognizes Rokesmith as Harmon, and Bella comes to realize who it is she has married. Lightwood is in fact a link character, connecting the Harmon plot with the courtship of Lizzie Hexam by his friend Eugene Wrayburn. Initially 'courtship' is too strong a word, and in the jargon of today he 'fancies' her at their first meeting by the riverside. Eugene is part of superior society, Lizzie of working-class respectability, and consequently these two aspects of the plot – the Veneerings and their society parasites on the one hand, and their contacts with the waterfront/dolls' dressmaker/schoolmaster on the other, indicate the range of the social concerns within the novel. Through Lizzie we meet Jenny Wren; through Lizzie's brother Charley we meet Bradley Headstone, who quickly becomes obsessed with Lizzie. In his mad jealousy Bradley ultimately attacks Wrayburn and almost kills him; then Bradley himself dies in mortal combat with Rogue Riderhood. The hangers-on of the Veneerings, such as the verbose and condescending Podsnap, the sickly-comic Lammles and the despicable Fascination Fledgeby, all underline Dickens's close moral castigation of the corruption existing in the higher levels of society. They provide a telling contrast with Betty Higden at the other end of 'society' – and with Jenny Wren for that matter too – where sincerity and a certain integrity are the keys to pride and social responsibility. The chapter summaries will indicate the further reaches of the plot – for example, the role played by the Wilfer family – but the main outline, which is concerned with John Harmon and the inheritance, has been indicated above.

Structure, themes and the principles of unity

Our Mutual Friend is one of the most complex of Dickens's works. The river and the Mounds – water and dust – are at the centre of it all, and the multiple associations of which these two are the pivot radiate through the plot. But no simple equation is possible here. The river takes away (Hexam, Headstone, Rogue Riderhood); in a sense it also releases (John Harmon and Eugene Wrayburn). Similarly the mounds corrupt, as in Wegg's case, but they also promote natural generosity, as seen in the Boffins and Bella and, indeed, in 'Rokesmith'. Society stigmatizes and reduces, as illustrated by the execrable Lammles, Fledgeby, Podsnap and the Veneerings; at the same time a particular voice of society echoes the degrees of integrity present in Lightwood, Eugene and, finally, Twemlow.

Our Mutual Friend is no 'loose, baggy monster', to use Henry James's famous dictum on 19th-century fiction, but a finely-structured work of art. Contrast and parallel are inherent in the plot. The incomplete proverbs in the headings of the four Books – The Cup and the Lip, Birds of a Feather, A Long Lane, A Turning – are deliberate emphases in the unravelling. 'There's many a slip,' indeed, for John Harmon, 'flock together' defines the coteries of Bradley and Charley, Lizzie and Jenny and Riah, Lammles, Veneerings, Podsnaps. The final two books are indissolubly linked anyway as the plot unfolds.

The title, too, should be considered. Rokesmith is 'Our Mutual Friend', but to Wegg and Venus Boffin is *their* mutual friend, and Riah is the mutual friend of Jenny and Lizzie. In an unpleasant and reverse way the Lammles and Fledgeby are mutual friends, as are Podsnaps and Veneerings and, in a curious and frightening atmosphere, this applies to Bradley Headstone and Rogue Riderhood.

This interpretation of the various layers of the plot works at a number of levels, all of which indicate a disciplined, imaginative sense of form, richly pleasing to the reader. The titles of the chapters themselves have linking points of cross-reference and association; thus the 'bird of prey' is directly associated, first, with Gaffer Hexam, then, by analogy, with Rogue Riderhood. Yet if we examine the distribution of the characters we are aware of other birds of prey: Wegg (on Boffin), Bradley Headstone (on Eugene), Fledgeby (on everyone with whom he comes into contact), the Lammles (on Georgiana), the Veneerings (on society), Lady Tippins (on whoever will listen to her); Podsnap, too, who preys on Providence, Venus, who obliquely preys on the dead.

There are curious parallels and analogies (one is reminded of the chapter called 'Minders and Re-minders', itself the definitive title for the method of *Our Mutual Friend*). Take the descriptions of Veneerings and Podsnaps at table, where camels and desert are presided over by the Analytical Chemist, a kind of dust contractor who has already sifted the valuables of the company. Here the principle of unity is clear. It has other variants: Boffin's Bower, that euphemistically named adjunct to the mounds, has a real but equally ironic equivalent when Riah sells waste cheaply to Jenny Wren. The description is peculiarly evocative when one thinks of other contexts in the novel:

> A few boxes of humble flowers and evergreens completed the garden; and the encompassing wilderness of dowager old chimneys twirled their cowls and fluttered their smoke, rather as if they were bridling, and fanning themselves, and looking on in a state of airy surprise. (Book 2, Chapter 5, p.332)

It seems odd to find society echoes almost reminiscent of Lady Tippins (dowagers, fluttered, bridling, fanning) where we would least expect it. It is even more surprising to consider the actual words used by Jenny to Riah and to Fledgeby, 'Come back, and be dead! Come back, and be dead!' (2,5,334). Obviously she is in heaven, and there is almost a reflection of Rossetti's Blessed Damozel when we read that Jenny was 'looking down out of a Glory of her long bright radiant hair'; the implications of her spoken words echo throughout the book like a literary acrostic. Better to be 'dead', says the author in commentary, than to be part of this mortal dust, this moral Mound of life that has become degradation for so many. Human love transcending the present appears to be the only thing worth having; what Jenny describes is a golden age of innocence in which the small garden on the roof-top is 'death' only because it is so much nearer heaven than the bottom of the river or the cramped conditions with her drunken child.

Eugene, for all his flippancy, realizes that Jenny's vision is one of innocence and goodness, true gold compared with the dross he has lived by. It is significant, too, that Betty Higden ends up close to heaven, the flowers and the greenery surrounding her death contrasting poignantly with the death of poor Dolls borne on his stretcher through the streets where he has cadged his last 'three penn'worth' of rum.

Jenny provides a running commentary on the nature of the society we view; in making dolls for the children of that society she is underlining its essential egocentricity. The miniatures are exact representations of society itself, just as the mirror and plate at the Veneerings reflect the glittering superficial nature of the company.

In his Postscript In Lieu of Preface dated 2 September 1865, Dickens sufficiently established the principles of unity to be found in *Our Mutual Friend*. When we remember that the book was published in monthly parts, like most of his other major fiction, we should perhaps look at the whole of the relevant paragraph:

To keep for a long time unsuspected, yet always working itself out, another purpose originating in that leading incident, and turning it to a pleasant and useful account at last, was at once the most interesting and the most difficult part of my design. Its difficulty was much enhanced by the mode of publication; for, it would be very unreasonable to expect that many readers, pursuing a story in portions from month to month through nineteen months, will, until they have it before them complete, perceive the relations of its finer threads to the whole pattern which is always before the eyes of the story-weaver at his loom. (Postscript, p.893)

We suffer from no such disadvantages, having the whole thing before us, thus being in a position to assess the detail of its structure. The central theme is money and everything associated with it – business, politics, greed, the poverty-line. Again the effect of the interaction is apparent. The Lammles have much in common with Wegg, since the aim of all three is the acquisition of money and, given the opportunity, the Lammles would have blackmailed Podsnap as Wegg intends to blackmail Boffin.

The river of life becomes also the river of death, the gold in the Mounds is also the dust to which we all return; the irony in the name Harmony Jail is also present when the bequest of a wicked man – a marriage contract based on money – becomes a marriage of love based on just that. Some arms of the law are indolent (Lightwood and Wrayburn) and some are active (Mr Inspector and his satellites); in the event, both are wrong-headed for a time. A ballad-monger with a wooden leg reads the *Decline and Fall* to an illiterate rich man, while the society parallel to them, and supposedly above them, traces its own decline and fall. Here even the details emphasize the mutuality of *Our Mutual Friend*: the ballad-monger occasionally drops into poetry as he ingratiates himself with his benefactor; Eugene Wrayburn and Lady Tippins play at life through a series of quotations and literary echoes. Lightwood and Wrayburn have lodgings in the empty Temple – while the Podsnappian Temple fails to provide a shrine for the 'young person', or indeed for any society acolytes. Linking all these is money – share prices, money-lending, even a market in human flesh to meet the need of the Boffins:

> The market was 'rigged' in various artful ways. Counterfeit stock got into circulation. Parents boldly represented themselves as dead, and brought their orphans with them. Genuine orphan-stock was surreptitiously withdrawn from the market . . . fluctuations of a wild and South-sea nature were occasioned, by orphan-holders keeping back, and then rushing into the market a dozen together. But, the uniform principle at the root of all these various operations was bargain and sale; and that principle could not be recognized by Mr & Mrs Milvey. (1,16,244)

In the above the Dickensian principle of unity in structure is exemplified yet again; this is the mighty world of high finance mirrored in the insignificant world of petty profit, a swingeing attack on the principle and the system from Podsnap to Wegg. Even 'Parents boldly represented themselves as dead' has its particular echo for us: the leading character in the novel has relinquished his own identity and is in the process of discovering for himself the quality of human (not material) gain that is likely to be his.

The central focus is on a society that has declined and fallen; and obviously human love (Lizzie), compassion and right-thinking (John Harmon), altruistic love and action (Betty Higden), and simple generosity (the Boffins) are the reforming forces needed to restore to that society humanitarian values and practice. From Marine Insurance to the administration of the Poor Law is no great leap – the guiding motive, which is money at the expense of the diminishing of the human spirit, is manifestly there. But any unity, or principle of relationships that embodies themes within its structure, is ultimately dependent on the styles employed by the writer. Some have been mentioned above, but a fuller guide is given in the section that follows.

Style

Dickens is the great independent stylist, so much so that his imitators, contemporaries with an eye to the main chance, were quick to translate him to stage and burlesque. Only one of the full-scale imitators – G. W. M. Reynolds – has survived, and a glance at his *Pickwick Abroad* indicates the difficulty of sustaining anything for any time in the Dickensian mode. We read (from *Pickwick Abroad*):

> and had not Mr Weller given his revered and respected master a compulsive and impelling shove behind, it is more than probable that Mr Pickwick would have remained standing at the bottom of the ladder till the arrival of the high tide should have enabled him to step on shore, by raising the vessel to a level with the quay.

The individual ebullience of Dickens is totally lacking here, the comic position of Mr Pickwick almost thrown away by the balance and seriousness of the style. Dickens was rightly called 'The Inimitable' in his own day.

Although we may feel that *Our Mutual Friend* is morbid in general outline, it is imbued with humour, sudden fresh and unusual, as when Bella bemoans the fact that Ma is always playing 'The Tragic Muse with a face-ache in majestic corners', or where the same lady is described as being 'majestically faint, and with a condescending stitch in her side'. Dickens's humour indeed assumes a variety of styles in this novel; for example, there is whimsy in using the image of the monastery in describing police investigations into the death of John Harmon. It is still whimsy, though of a different kind, that has the whole process of financial manipulation, share-buying and selling and the maintenance of a financial establishment, expressed in terms of the Fathers of the Church. Strange that in both instances a spiritual dimension is being conveyed where there is certainly no spiritual context; but if the laugh is rueful it is also highly moral.

In Dickens, satire and irony are the twin weapons of castigation, but there is a variety of tone, and of seriousness, in their particular usages. The whole of the 'bran-new' sequence – which categorizes the Veneerings at their first dinner party, and the description of Lady Tippins as a 'hardy old cruiser' – gives way, by the time we get to the wedding of the Lammles, to near slapstick:

For he, standing on the doorsteps to grace the departure, is suddenly caught a most prodigious thump on the side of his head with a heavy shoe, which a Buffer in the hall, champagne-flushed and wild of aim, has borrowed on the spur of the moment from the pastrycook's porter, to cast after the departing pair as an auspicious omen. (1,10,168)

The Analytical (the ancient retainer) is thus made to look ridiculous; but brooding over this chapter is the mordant humour that defines the loveless/mercenary motives of Alfred and Sophronia – linked, as always, with another situation ever present in the reader's mind; this chapter is called 'A Marriage Contract', and we think of John Harmon and Bella.

Podsnap is the particular recipient of Dickensian irony; habit is eternally scorned through the dance, which is a related kind of ritual, where we are told that:

sixteen disciples of Podsnappery went through the figures of – 1, Getting up at eight and shaving close at a quarter past – 2, Breakfasting at nine – 3, Going to the City at ten – 4, Coming home at half-past five – 5, Dining at seven, and the grand chain. (1,11,184)

This factual and habitual employment is seen as being equivalent to the rote learning of educational facts, or the rote application of business affairs.

Sometimes the author can be sly: while revealing little Miss Peecher's visions of herself and Bradley Headstone, he tells us that in the background 'the nightingales tuned up'. This humour is at the expense of romance; but verbal humour is present throughout *Our Mutual Friend*: from the 'young rocking horse' which describes Georgiana, to the 'Alfred David' which Riderhood is prepared to swear. A running humour is also present, for example, in songs and music; Bella frequently reverts to the Dead March in Saul, Marine Insurance's particular gift to Providence is seen in the parody 'See the conquering Podsnap comes', but best of all are the ballads and adaptations of Silas Wegg. Consider Boffin's Bower, and Wegg's rendering of 'Home, Sweet Home' (with not a little pathos).

There is, of course, particular significance in the choice of Riderhood as a name; but then almost all the names in Dickens repay a second look. 'Wilfer' with its associations of wilfulness, certainly applies to three of the family, and the sound of names like Boffin, Wegg, Lammle is roughly definitive of the types of people they are. Jenny Wren's diminutive sharpness is well conveyed, while Headstone has the composite morbidity and dullness which we associate with tombstones and with the Victorian schoolmaster. Twemlow is an indeterminate name for an indeterminate person, and Dickens obviously enjoys using him as the focus of some of his enlightening comment in the novel. Early on, this comment is sympathetic:

> For, the poor little harmless gentleman once had his fancy, like the rest of us, and she didn't answer (as she often does not), and he thinks the adorable bridesmaid is like the fancy as she was then (which she is not at all).(1,10,164)

This relationship between author and reader is one of the hallmarks of Victorian fiction, as we can see from a glance at Thackeray, Trollope, George Eliot and Mrs Gaskell – and in Charlotte Bronte's final confidence in *Jane Eyre*, 'Reader, I married him.' Once again Dickens displays his range; he cares for Twemlow like a parent, and three hundred pages later we find him addressing his fictional child in mock-pathetic tones:

Ah! my Twemlow! Say, little feeble grey personage, what thoughts are in thy breast today, of the Fancy – so still to call her who bruised thy heart. (2,16,467)

Often authorial comment is reinforced, as here, by repetition, so that Dickens's indictment of the maladministration of the Poor Law occurs in text whenever Betty Higden is present, becoming almost like the refrain of a song:

Absolutely impossible my Lords and Gentlemen and Honourable Boards, by any stretch of legislative wisdom to set these perverse people right in their logic? (1,16,248)

This appears much later with the question answered, but here it takes on that unifying function which we notice so often in *Our Mutual Friend*:

My lords and gentlemen and honourable boards, when you in the course of your dust-shovelling and cinder-raking have piled up a mountain of pretentious failure, you must off with your honourable coats for the removal of it, and fall to the work with the power of all the queen's horses and all the queen's men, or it will come rushing down and bury us alive. (3,8,565)

The relationship to the central theme of money and its associated corruption; the connection with the Mounds; the decline and fall of society: all are embodied in this image. Consequently the author's own voice here is diffuse, for the central focus at this time is Betty Higden; though the wider implications of the suffering of one poor lady are evident too. Sometimes the voice identifies closely with the action, so that when Lightwood and Mr Inspector are in the public house we are told that 'We got hot brandy and water, and it revived us wonderfully.'

Often the comment is moral in tone and, having described

the nature of Bradley Headstone, Dickens applies his observations generally:

As a multitude of weak, imitative natures are always lying by, ready to go mad upon the next wrong idea that may be broached – in these times, generally some form of tribute to Somebody for something that never was done, or, if ever done, that was done by Somebody Else – so these less ordinary natures may lie by for years, ready on the touch of an instant to burst into flame (2,11,396)

Personification is widely used in *Our Mutual Friend*, and sometimes it has very strong symbolic suggestions. Consider this description, as Lizzie waits for the return of her father on the day she has persuaded Charley to leave home:

The white face of the winter day came sluggishly on, veiled in a frosty mist; and the shadowy ships in the river slowly changed to black substances; and the sun, blood-red on the eastern marshes behind dark masts and yards, seemed filled with the ruins of a forest it had set on fire. (1,6,118)

Now in mood and suggestibility this day *is* Lizzie, and the scene is fraught with her suffering and foreboding. 'Shadowy', 'black', 'blood-red' all carry associations of death: for her father, and for the near-death of Eugene. The 'ruins of a forest . . . set on fire' reflects the destructive natures of both Charley and Bradley Headstone. Here, in complete contrast, is another, again the river as symbol:

the young river, dimpled like a young child, playfully gliding away among the trees, unpolluted by the defilements that lie in wait for it on its course, and as yet out of hearing of the deep summons of the sea. (3,8,567)

All this is appropriate to Betty Higden on her journey, but once more the overtones are strongly suggestive. The mention of the 'young child' recalls Betty's delight in looking after children, but 'unpolluted by defilements' registers even more sharply, since it implies the 'defilement' of the Poor Law administration, while the 'deep summons of the sea' is the call to death. This, Betty's last journey, is her own hearing of that call. But if the river is a symbol for both the good and the evil in life, then public education is the symbol for all that is turgid and without life, the reduction to Facts (which had been heavily attacked some ten years earlier in *Hard Times*). When Charley Hexam and Bradley set out on one occasion to meet Lizzie, Miss Peecher and Mary Anne indulge in the following dialogue:

'When you say *they* say, what do you mean? Part of speech They?'
Mary Anne hooked her right arm behind her in her left hand, as being under examination, and replied:
'Personal pronoun.'
'Person, They?'
'Third person.'
'Number, They?'
'Plural number.' (2,1,270)

The satire is keen-edged; Dickens is far more concerned with the education of the character and the personality than with any formal, limiting appraisal.

At times he anticipates the development of the English novel. In the chapter 'A Solo and a Duett', for example, John Harmon's revelations about himself are a 'stream of consciousness'. But Dickens was passionately fond of theatricals, and the revelations begin as a soliloquy of the theatre, with the reader as audience. The scene in which the Lammles are endeavouring to involve Georgiana and Fledgeby is pure theatrical satire. Since their marriage is a long-running performance, the language used to describe their machinations is appropriate: Alfred is 'like a harlequin'; 'Mrs Lammle took the prompt-book.' Alfred returns to the attack, for 'The Manager had put him down in the bill for the part and he must play it.'

Humour of various kinds, satire, irony, a wide use of image and symbol, the variant nature of his own voice, are Dickens's modes of expression in *Our Mutual Friend*. Those that have hardly found mention here because of limited space will be referred to in the textual notes.

Characters

John Harmon

The dark gentleman. Thirty at the utmost. An expressive, one might say handsome, face. A very bad manner. In the last degree constrained, reserved, diffident, troubled. His eyes were on Miss Bella for an instant, and then looked at the ground as he addressed the master of the house. (1,4,81)

'Our mutual friend' of the title is the heir to the Harmon estate. Drugged and thrown into the Thames on the way home to claim his inheritance, he survives, and acts as the moral yardstick of the novel. Since the Harmon fortune has been bequeathed to him on condition that he marries Bella Wilfer, Julius Handford (alias John Rokesmith, really John Harmon) is able, as secretary to Mr Boffin, to observe Bella at close hand.

The Harmon role is certainly more rooted in the theatre than in real life. We are asked to believe that John influences Mr Boffin to join in the deception and that he persuades Bella to marry him after having put her uncompromisingly to the test without revealing his secret. This is alien to both their characters, and is far more the substance of melodrama than of reality. John Harmon is capable of an almost professional standard of acting – witness his interview first with Pleasant and then with Rogue Riderhood. It is only in Chapters 12 and 13 of Book 2 that he comes positively to life through his determination to make Rogue sign the paper that will lift the stigma from Lizzie.

There follows his proposal to Bella and his long narrative – revealing what really happened to him and explaining his motives in remaining 'dead'. There is some fine psychological casework here; he remains, nevertheless, his author's mouthpiece, rather cloying in his (to the reader) known goodness.

Rokesmith, as he is referred to for most of the action, buries himself beneath figurative mounds of right conduct, which complement the physical mounds which are rightfully his. He is greatly compassionate to Betty Higden; ensures that Johnny gets the toys and is taken to hospital; and goes to the little boy like a good angel on the night of his death. He is equally protective and concerned for Sloppy; and ensures that Betty carries a letter that will identify her in time of need, thus protecting her from the degradation of Poor Law burial. He is unfailingly courteous and considerate to Mrs Boffin, and tolerant of the 'wilful' Bella and the perversely wilful Mrs Wilfer. He is every bit as worthy as the early Dickensian heroines, and one cannot entirely believe him capable of sustaining the deception of 'Rokesmith' for so long.

Rokesmith is not so much a character as a moral way of life, and prior to his marriage there is very little evidence of a sense of humour. Although he avoids Mortimer Lightwood for fear of being recognized, he is self-possessed (much more so than Mortimer) when they confront each other in a London street (4,12,827). He is incredibly self-assured when he is 'arrested' by Mr Inspector; he enjoys his own shocking effect on Potterson and Kibble; he indulges his anger with Silas Wegg on Mr Boffin's account – yet he never comes alive in a full-blooded way. Upright, kindly, but compelled to play a part, he seldom emerges from the tangle of the plot as a true character.

Bella

Bella . . . with her brown eyes on the fire and a handful of her brown curls in her mouth, laughed at this, and then pouted and half cried. (1,4,79)

Bella is one of the most attractive of Dickens's heroines, partly because she is flawed early and grows in character (though not always convincingly) as the plot unfolds. Dickens's previous novel was *Great Expectations* (1860–71), and Bella marks a major advance on Estella, the near-anti-heroine, and Biddy, with her wholesome, uncomplicated common sense. Bella gives every promise of being petulant and thoroughly tiresome, but the psychological background to her wayward, essentially spoiled nature is convincing enough.

Mrs Wilfer lives in a state of perpetual siege, victim of her own self-pity, but with considerable histrionic compensations which are also present in Bella. Lavvy resembles her mother and Bella in her ability to dramatize a situation, while R. Wilfer is the cherub, warm and affectionate, which Bella also is to become.

Bella does, in fact, turn out to be a delightful character. Independent and strong-willed, with a family to escape from, she predictably sets her sights on a wealthy marriage. Hitherto her one outlet has been her love for her father, but then she is treated kindly by the unpolished Mrs Boffin, and witnesses suffering in the persons of Betty Higden, Johnny and Sloppy. As a result of these experiences Bella's false pride is transformed, her feelings are educated and softened, and she becomes increasingly aware of the worth of John Rokesmith. Impetuosity gives way to reflection; she knows that she has been unkind in her treatment of the Secretary, and she has the character to remonstrate with Mr Boffin – and this despite her love for Mrs Boffin – on his supposedly unjust treatment of Rokesmith. With the latter dismissed, Bella dismisses herself and goes off to share bread and milk with her father, the simple fare symbolizing her rejection of riches. The arrival of Rokesmith in pursuit of his 'courageous girl' forces upon her the welcome knowledge that she loves him. 'Courageous' is the right word for Bella, for she chooses to abandon the mercenary part of herself that would have eliminated all warmth from her nature.

What *is* difficult to accept is the ease with which Bella is deceived by John, for she is intelligent and intuitive, and one would expect her to ask more questions than she does. Her return home after her marriage is a triumph, for she has learned something of humility and tolerance; and her acceptance of the family she had once found so trying is a mark of maturity. Bella as cook, needlewoman, and idyllically happy with the Inexhaustible, belongs to the world of romance; she has married her Prince Charming, despite her own rebellion at being type-cast as Cinderella.

Lizzie Hexam

Lizzie took her right hand from the scull it held, and touched her lips with it, and for a moment held it out lovingly towards him. (1,1,46)

Perhaps the real Cinderella is Lizzie, seen in the above quotation with her father as he plies his trade and she helps him to raise the dead from the river. Ironically, at the moment of supreme crisis, Lizzie is intent on raising the beloved near-dead Eugene, giving him the selfless devotion and strength she had once given her father. It is Lizzie's finest hour, extended into weeks of agony, as she watches at the bedside of the man she loves.

Lizzie has a good deal in common with Rose Maylie of *Oliver Twist*, and with Little Dorrit herself, for she is intrinsically *good*. She wants education for her brother, and sees his future in 'the hollow by the flare'. She loves her father despite his trade, fears for him and defends him; makes friends with the crippled dolls' dressmaker; and rejects the overtures of the unsuitable and physically repugnant Bradley Headstone. She makes her own refuge in the roof garden with Jenny; has for Riah the natural respect that he merits; and is conveniently on hand to sweeten – angelically – the last moments of Betty Higden. But Lizzie has a fine spirit, and will not countenance any cheapness in her relationship with her gentleman suitor.

She rejects, too, her beloved Charley for what he has become in his total selfishness.

Lizzie does not breathe the same air as Bella but the early scenes with her father and Charley, and her shy acknowledgement of Eugene's interest in her, are realistic, though later she is to become much more an idea than an actuality. We must return to her saving of Eugene; for here, in frustrating the vengeance of her former suitor, she comes back to life. Dickens conveys the greater-than-human strength that possesses her, and it is a tribute to the early presentation of her character that we find her convincing in these anguished actions.

Eugene Wrayburn

You wouldn't marry for some money and some station, because you were frightfully likely to become bored. Are you less frightfully likely to become bored, marrying for no money and no station? (4,6,765)

The above quotation holds the key to Eugene (in so far as anything does) prior to the murderous assault on him by Bradley Headstone. He is an indolent young man who enjoys his own satirical slant on society. As a barrister he has no clients, and shows little sign of acquiring any. He lacks direction and is forever pondering on what 'M.R.F.' would say – hence the dialogue at the head of this section.

Wrayburn meets Lizzie through the Harmon affair and his friend Lightwood's initial involvement (via Mr Inspector) in it. He is attracted to her, though acutely aware of the class difference. Despite his flippancy he is sensitive, for he makes no attempt to seduce Lizzie though her image haunts his mind. In the face of Charley's objections (and his setting up Bradley as Lizzie's would-be teacher) Eugene has her educated (with Jenny). To Bradley he is contemptuous to the extent of refusing to address him by name, preferring to stigmatize him as 'Schoolmaster'.

Even in his bewilderment about Lizzie, he recognizes her character and her worth – and in this he reacts sharply against the class divisions of his own society. One of the most significant actions in Eugene's life is the sending of Mortimer to fetch Jenny Wren. He talks to Jenny of her own visions of flowers, birds and children, realizing that in her vision of innocence lies his own salvation. It is Jenny alone who understands intuitively that he wishes to marry Lizzie. This is his reparation: Lizzie has saved his life, and he dedicates his to her; though we may feel there is a certain selfishness in his decision, the fact remains that Eugene has rejected the worthless society of the past. He refuses to run away from that society to the colonies, promising Lizzie that he will work and support her.

While Eugene may not be altogether convincing as a character, he is an interesting departure – as is Bella – from the conventional lover. He learns through suffering; pettiness vanishes, and in his shattered body he finds a new soul.

Silas Wegg

a man with a wooden leg had sat for some years, with his remaining foot in a basket in cold weather . . . All weathers saw the man at the post. (1,5,87)

Silas Wegg is the genuine Dickensian eccentric. Just as all the characters in the novel have some kind of moral measure, so Wegg is no exception. His stall is near Cavendish Square; his ballad-mongery gives him a delightful facility in quotation (both accurate and inaccurate); frequently with individual humorous embellishments. Disappointingly, beneath this is a man devoured by greed. Treated generously by Mr Boffin, he is determined to get as much as he can out of his benefactor. He does indeed require the sustenance – beginning with the pie and continuing thereafter with gin and water – for those marathon readings from *The Decline and Fall of the Roman Empire* and the *Lives and Anecdotes of Misers*. There is, too, a wide streak of vengeance in his nature, which will have its way. His relationship with Venus – his anti-Rokesmith self-protection society – leads to his confiding his discovery of the later-dated Harmon Will. Thereafter he regards the Mounds and everything accruing from them as his own property, and takes malicious pleasure in the humbling and blackmailing of Boffin. Unknown to him, Venus – his own affairs with Pleasant Riderhood assisted by Rokesmith and Boffin – reveals the truth to the Golden Dustman; and Wegg's triumph becomes his humiliation. He has shown himself to be a scavenger and is eventually 'helped' into a scavenger's cart by Sloppy.

The money theme is exemplified at its lowest social level by Wegg; but there is a pathetic element too in his nature, born of loneliness and deprivation. He fills the house opposite with people; his greed as custodian of the Bower leaves him a physical wreck. His rendering of ballads is a joy, his villainy larger than life. In many respects he is the moral antithesis of Betty Higden: she lives to help others; Wegg to batten on to them. Greater humanity would have helped him to derive much benefit from the company of Mr Boffin.

Mr Boffin

a broad, round-shouldered, one-sided fellow in mourning, coming comically ambling towards the corner, dressed in a pea over-coat, and carrying a large stick . . . but with bright, eager, childishly-enquiring, grey eyes. (1,5,90)

Boffin is delightful caricature and again exemplifies the theatrical mode of presentation. Like Harmon he has to play a part for much of the novel. A genuine eccentric, we know of his kindness in the past to young John Harmon. What *is* remarkable is the fact that such a man should be capable of tolerating the repugnant character of his employer at Harmony Jail. His inheritance of £100,000 makes him the Golden Dustman. This gives him the leisure to acquire fashion (largely on Mrs Boffin's account), and learning (entirely on his own), resulting in the appointment of Wegg.

Some critical appraisal of Boffin has regarded him as not only near-illiterate but also as someone easily duped: in view of the fact that he successfully 'dupes' Bella, this is hard to credit. It seems, too, that having adopted Bella and recognized John Harmon, he is just as intent on testing human nature as John is. His great kindness is demonstrated by his generosity to Wegg, his willingness to help his wife in the pursuit of an orphan, and Bella's affection for him.

The deception entered into by Harmon and himself leads to the exposure of human nature in the way they wish: namely, the integrity of Bella (who rejects the unacceptable face of miserly stricture); the cunning of the parasitic Lammles; and the greed of Wegg.

In essence, Boffin represents simplicity, goodness and generosity in the face of temptation. His reactions to his changed circumstances are almost naive. When the mounds are carted away Boffin is, so to speak, cleared of his dust and of all that adheres to it, including his 'changed' character. He resumes the good and unpretentious life that is his own.

Mrs Boffin

Mrs Boffin who, perpetually smiling, had approached and drawn her plump arm through her lord's, most willingly complied. Fashion, in the form of her black velvet hat and feathers, tried to prevent it; but got deservedly crushed in the endeavour. (1,5,101)

Mrs Boffin too is a simple and kindly soul. Boffin's Bower in the shadow of the Mounds gives way to her becoming a 'high-flyer' at Fashion, to quote her husband's fond and totally inaccurate view of his spouse. She is goodness personified. Simple working-class characters are among Dickens's strengths, and Mrs Boffin's description of the childhood of John Harmon and his sister, her preservation of their childish scrawl, and her joy when she discovers who John really is, are evidence of her warmth and sympathy.

Like her husband 'Noddy', she is an eccentric, particularly in speech; again we are asked to accept the fact that she too takes part in the deception, though it is later revealed (with great sentiment) that she and 'Noddy' were concealed in the church when Bella and John were married. Her desire to adopt an orphan is further indication of her goodness – again there is an interesting focus on the childless couple who adopt their own children (John, Bella, Sloppy, little Johnny).

R. Wilfer

If the conventional Cherub could ever grow up and be clothed, he might be photographed as a portrait of Wilfer. His chubby, smooth, innocent appearance was a reason for his being always treated with condescension when he was not put down. (1,4,75)

R. Wilfer is not merely a 'Cherub', he is the prototype henpecked husband (some of Dickens's portraits of marriage are somewhat embittered at this period). In the eyes of his wife he lacks drive and ambition. Rumty's Perch is indicative of his place and his status; it is one of Mrs Wilfer's sustained rhetorical flourishes that she was destined to marry a tall man (Frederick of Prussia's Potsdam guards are mentioned in this context). None the less, Rumty has his own attributes. He is balanced, understandably a little melancholy, and dearly loves his daughter Bella; indeed, he tolerates her fussing with remarkable patience. He is devoid of the histrionics or self-indulgence that characterize his wife and daughters.

But Wilfer too (albeit with the machinations of Bella) is

forced to act a part. He is the downtrodden clerk in fact, lifted by his daughter's romance, but opting out of the inevitable altercation by dozing off in a crisis. It is his defence against the excessive demands of the temperaments and tempers of others. He is essentially good and, as his daughter's confidant, his influence has, we feel, been responsible for counteracting her mercenary streak. Bella's education really began at home where her kind and long-suffering father helped to teach her what matters – in the light, alas, of his own experience.

Mrs Wilfer

a tall woman and angular ... necessarily majestic ... She was much given to tying up her head in a pocket-handkerchief, knotted under the chin ... (invariably assuming it when in low spirits or difficulties), and as a species of full dress. (1,4,77)

Majestic, histrionic, always acting for her family audience, Mrs Wilfer is an outstanding eccentric. She is dominating and tries to remain so, but is occasionally overtaken by her own self-dramatization, and is accordingly reduced. She is never pleasant; everyone within orbit suffers the range of her self-pity, which is generally dredged up from the past and the vast areas of might-have-been. She can be relied upon to milk any situation of its dramatic potential: thus, the first appearance of Rokesmith as the new lodger occasions her misery on account of a loss of independence (the possible setting up of a small private school).

Although it would be untrue to say that Mrs Wilfer enjoys any aspect of life, she is undoubtedly at her best in adversity: since she spends her life finding cause for complaint, adversity is the spur to both morbid and nostalgic self-indulgence. She is the tragedy queen in a life too petty for tragedy, with a keen sense of inverted snobbery. It is significant, for example, that she trusts neither John Rokesmith nor Mr Boffin, resenting the patronage of the latter. The reader should note her performance in the first scene and, more particularly, on the return of Bella after her marriage. Despite Mrs Wilfer's resentment of patronage, she manages to exercise it throughout with all the artistry of the (in her own eyes) undervalued woman.

Lavvy

Lavvy has not known the trial that Bella has known. (1,4,79)

Lavvy is the younger sister, with sufficient of her mother's capacity for self-indulgence to be in a constant state of war with everybody. She is jealous of Bella (and probably of the married sister Cecilia, whose nobility and sacrifice are held up by their mother as examples to her other daughters), sneers at her parents, and leads her affianced George Sampson a dog's life; he is, however, a cast-off suitor of Bella's – so, like her mother, she is making do with second-best. She is perpetually ill-humoured, constantly sniping, for she has also inherited her mother's flair for unpleasant innuendo. The wonder is that George Sampson puts up with her, since between Lavinia and her mother he is verbally tossed from pillar to post. Lavvy has her part in the Cinderella aspect of the Bella plot: her looks are not stressed, but she is cast as one of the ugly sisters.

Bradley Headstone

his decent black coat and waistcoat, and decent white shirt, and decent formal black tie, and decent pantaloons of pepper and salt, with his decent silver watch in his pocket . . . looked a thoroughly decent young man of six-and-twenty. (11, 1,266)

This 'highly certificated stipendiary schoolmaster' is the real villain of the novel, since his 'decent' exterior cannot hide his violently passionate feelings. His features tremble and become contorted; blood spurts from his nose; his questions of the Reverend Frank Milvey lead to what is described as a fit. Just as he raises Charley, so he raises himself, despite the stigma of birth, but Dickens uses him in further sense, for he represents in his slavish adherence to ritual learning Dickens's central attack on the educational system of the time. Bradley has neither flair nor imagination; the irrational element in his love for Lizzie, and his temptation towards the sensual he has so guarded against are an indictment of the nature of learning and the repression it brings with it.

His irrationality is shown too in his hatred for Eugene. Here is the class division, for Eugene is inescapably a gentleman, whereas Bradley is not. Respectability sits uneasily on such a passionate nature, and after his humiliation at the hands of Eugene, and at the gentler but equally firm hands of Lizzie, his course is fairly charted. Again this involves some unifying of the plot devices: Bradley Headstone, like John Harmon and Mr Boffin, has an extra role to play – that of a bargeman. It is an elaborate role and reflects the extent of his monomania, but Rogue Riderhood sees through it and thus brings about both their deaths.

Bradley, however, is not a completely one-sided character; we are out of sympathy with him because we are aware of the danger of his capacity to ignite (without and within), but his rejection by Lizzie, and his own awareness of what his love for her has done to him, makes him a pathetic figure. In effect he is psychologically very well drawn; we feel for him when he learns that Lizzie is to be married to Eugene Wrayburn, and when Rogue Riderhood makes his appearance in the schoolroom; and we marvel at his strength of will and his superhuman stamina. We cannot forgive him his cowardly attack upon Eugene but like the author, we too cannot forgive the society that produced him. There is a subtle edge to his presentation: we have noted his epileptic tendencies, but we should also recognize his schizophrenic ones and record once more Dickens's astute insight into the dark reaches of the human personality.

Jesse Hexam

a strong man with ragged grizzled hair and a sun-browned face. (1,1,43)

After the initial chapters, Jesse hardly merits a mention. He searches the Thames for bodies, robbing them before he gives them to the police. He finds the body identified as that of John Harmon; he will have nothing to do with Rogue Riderhood, who calls him 'pardner', so that Rogue is quite willing to swear an 'Alfred David' that Gaffer killed the supposed Harmon. Before Hexam is found drowned near his own boat we find him involved in a scene with Lizzie over the departure of Charley, and for a dreadful moment he stands with a knife, appearing a murderer indeed to his terrified daughter. He is, however, kind and tender to her when he realizes the extent of her fear; but under no circumstances will he see Charley again.

Rogue Riderhood

a man with a squinting leer (1,1,46)

Riderhood, obviously to be associated with 'Ridinghood', is the wolf of the fairy story. He had been Gaffer Hexam's 'pardner', as he reminds him; but when he is rebuffed by Gaffer on the water he does his utmost to incriminate Hexam, both locally and with the law, so as to get his share of the reward money. This is the more ironic when we learn that Rogue himself was involved in the attack on the Harmon heir. He appears at different stages in the narrative, always intent on self-aggrandizement. He is overturned by a below-bridge steamer and very nearly drowned, those who resuscitate him clearing off quickly when he recovers.

He later becomes an assistant lock-keeper up the Thames in Oxfordshire; he misleads Betty Higden (which underlines his cruelty and unscrupulousness), then gets caught up in the strife between Bradley Headstone and Wrayburn. Rogue and Bradley meet outside Lightwood's office by accident; after walking together for a time, Bradley gives Rogue five shillings as an investment for the future. As a result Rogue watches Bradley's duplicity and his attempts to use him (Riderhood) as a cover for the crime by adopting his posture and his clothes. Rogue Riderhood realizes that Bradley Headstone has killed (or nearly killed) Wrayburn, and goes to the school; he then blackmails Bradley at the river lock. Bradley knows that he will never be able to shake off Riderhood, clasps him in an iron grip, and they sink to their death in the mud behind the lock-gates.

Fascination Fledgeby

feeling for his whiskers with his spoon, his wine glass, and his bread. (2,4,315)

Fascination Fledgeby is a moneylender and opportunist. He runs Pubsey and Co, and takes great delight in putting in the financial boot wherever possible, particularly when it results in bringing down a 'friend'. Riah is his mask, a patriarch disguised as an executioner, and is thus blamed for what the unscrupulous Fledgeby exacts – witness the suffering of Jenny Wren on account of her 'godmother's' corruption. Lammle stands to gain from him if he procures for Fledgeby the hand of Georgiana Podsnap, but that young lady is rescued by Mrs Lammle, via Twemlow. Fledgeby naturally takes it out on Lammle, who is more than a match for him, and gives him a violent beating after the Lammles have been sold up. Jenny arrives just after this, wraps Fledgeby in brown paper and vinegar – and includes a few grains of pepper!

Fledgeby has succeeded in involving Twemlow and Eugene

in his usury, but Mortimer Lightwood extricates both with the aid of the real John Harmon, whom he finally recognizes. Crafty, unscrupulous, with a taste for exotic bedroom wear, Fledgeby is a thoroughly distasteful character.

Other characters

Our Mutual Friend is richly peopled, but by reason of the multiple plot some characters come immediately alive while others develop slowly in the unravelling. *The Lammles* have a particular plot function, since they represent greed and the money theme in the society level of the plot. The Lammles, who are friends of the *Veneerings*, discover to their infinite cost (literally) that each has believed that in marrying the other he/she is marrying money. They learn this on their honeymoon, and determine to make the best of it by maintaining their precarious foothold on the rich, and making money out of them.

Alfred is infinitely the nastier of the two; totally without conscience, he delights in baiting his wife. Sophronia has a heart: not only does she save Georgiana from the machinations of her husband and herself, but when that warm and misguided girl stands by them in their adversity (and no one else in society does), Sophronia movingly thanks the Boffins for not betraying her husband and herself to Georgiana. Receiving a hundred pounds from the Boffins, they go abroad: society has rejected them. They are seen in contrast to Wrayburn and Lizzie, whom society would likewise reject, but Eugene is prepared to fight society's prejudices, on behalf of the wife he loves.

Mortimer Lightwood's role is that of link man. His one client is Mr Boffin, and consequently he is able on three occasions to recount to the Veneering dinner table the Harmon side of the plot from the very beginning. Society, though he is part of it, does not have a complete hold on him in the end: he now knows the truth about the Harmon affair; he has seen the beneficent influence of John and the Boffins; and, above all, the devotion to Eugene – in their separate ways – of Jenny Wren and Lizzie. He comes to encourage Eugene's marriage; and just as Eugene's suffering educates his feelings, so Lightwood's new awareness of the innate goodness of common humanity brings wisdom and maturity. Like Eugene, he determines to work in the future.

At somewhat more potent influence in this society is *Mr Podsnap*. His appearances are few, but his 'fatal freshness' is devastating in its complacency. He is in Marine Insurance, he believes in a Providence that is Podsnap, and for him British is not merely best but the only thing in existence – on one occasion his condescension to a French guest is insufferable.

The whole colouring of Podsnap is satirical – funny in the extreme because of the serious self-importance that marks his every utterance and even his every movement. Naturally, he puts a stop to the marrying off of Georgiana. Podsnap is misguided, boring, mean and altogether intolerable.

Georgiana exists as the young person: blushing, stammering, an object of attention solely because she is her father's daughter. She has an inherent decency of nature (as opposed to the contrived decency of Bradley Headstone), which causes her to respond to those she believes to be her friends, for instance the Lammles. This reveals her naivety. *Mrs Podsnap*, she of the 'rocking-horse's eye', is a large-featured, snobbish, insincere woman with little genuine feeling for her daughter Georgiana; she is shown to be an ideal wife for Mr Podsnap.

Twemlow is an important link character who represents the moral yardstick within society. He never knows whether or not he is an intimate friend of the Veneerings, but he is a gentleman born and bred, which is more than can be said for the Veneerings and their ilk with whom he is forced to associate. He is a cousin of Lord Snigsworth, which gives him an entrée to fashionable society. Twice in the course of the action he proves himself to be right-minded: he listens to Mrs Lammle, and this saves Georgiana from the clutches of Fledgeby; and he defends, in no uncertain terms, the right of Eugene Wrayburn to marry the woman he loves.

The *Veneerings* are merely classic society ciphers, climbing on to the political bandwagon as on to all others that can establish them in the right circles.

On this level of society, *Lady Tippins* is perhaps the most particularized, with her fiction about her lovers, her grotesque 'naughty' conversation. Her late husband was 'knighted in mistake for somebody else'. She represents the voice of society which Lightwood and Twemlow come to despise, and Eugene ignores. She is talkative, vain, superficial and wholly unsympathetic.

Charley Hexam is a depressing character. In the shared early days with Lizzie there is goodness in him, yet he makes no effort to prevent its being gradually driven out by the acquisition of learning and respectability. Charley represents self-love; he has inherited the bad in his father, Lizzie the good. He does not become a criminal, except in the spirit; his determination to advance results in the rejection of gratitude, naturalness and generosity of feeling.

Mr Venus is a most interesting caricature, with his loss in love (at least for the first part of our acquaintance with him), his 'Hindoo' baby in a bottle, his experiments in articulation and his moral control over Wegg, though unsuspected by the latter. There is a strange quality about the taxidermist – in a way he is bound to Wegg, for he has purchased the latter's leg. He is generally represented as 'floating in tea'. Pleasant Riderhood does not approve of his line of business but ultimately she is won over. Venus is a character who represents moral growth, since he gives up his part in the plot to bring down Boffin, and confides in the latter. Obviously, he takes great pride in his work.

Riah, the good Jew (in contrast to Fagin, the bad Jew of *Oliver Twist*), never comes alive. He is goodness personified, and if Jenny doubts him we cannot. But Fledgeby presents him as the merciless grasping Jew, and persuades everyone he can to agree with this. Riah stands by Lizzie (once in the face of Eugene), and finds her a place in the country. He later obtains his release from Fledgeby and makes his home with Jenny Wren as her lodger.

Mr Dolls, as Eugene calls him, appears only fitfully in the narrative; and is treated as a child by Jenny. Dolls gets Lizzie's address for Eugene, then drinks himself into a state of collapse and death.

Of the other male characters, *Mr Inspector* registers strongly in two scenes: the first when the identity of 'John Harmon' is established in death; the second when he waits for the real John Harmon, nearly arrests him but is nonplussed by the revelations; then takes John to see Kibble and Potterson.

Frank Milvey and *Mrs Milvey* come over as well-meaning, honest people, he 'wretchedly paid' but doing his best to find the genuine orphan the Boffins are looking for. He officiates at the wedding of Eugene and Lizzie, having inadvertently revealed to Bradley Headstone that it was about to take place. He also travels to conduct the simple funeral of *Betty Higden*. The latter is a devoted child-minder who lives in the past in the lives of the many children she has cared for, and in the Power and the Glory of the present and future which will keep her from Poor Law burial. She is nearly eighty years old; and Sloppy is required to do her mangling for her, a task he performs with great pride. Her long life of suffering is ended when she journeys independently, hoping to sell a few things, collapses but insists on going on. Lizzie finds her, and is with her at the end.

Sloppy is the orphan adopted by the Boffins and, appropriately, he carts away the Mounds – watched by the irate Wegg – whom he finally sends away on a rubbish cart! He is kind and understanding to *Jenny Wren.* The latter, whose real name is Fanny Cleaver, is a remarkable creation. Her love and loyalty to Lizzie, her care of her father and her whimsical but moving vision in the rooftop garden, all live in the reader's memory. She is crippled, far-seeing and astute, even though at one point she doubts Riah. She sees into the heart of a matter – witness her understanding of Eugene's wishes and needs – and into the nature of evil. She is sharp but warm, imaginative but practical, and her fantasies about her dolls take on reality for her. One wonders if her own responses to Sloppy will lead to their future life together.

Young Blight deals convincingly with Boffin early in the novel and carries an important message, while *Miss Peecher* and *Mary Anne* exist through their commentaries, voiced and unvoiced, on Bradley and Charley. *Pleasant Riderhood* survives her rogue father and lives, presumably in bliss, with Mr Venus, while *Abbey Potterson* will ensure the respectability – though not in the 'decent' sense – of the Six Jolly Fellowship Porters.

Chapter summaries and textual notes

Book 1 The Cup and the Lip

Chapter 1 On the Look Out

The short introductory chapter to the novel has father and daughter in a boat on the Thames: Lizzie is obviously apprehensive about their trade, which involves searching for bodies, money and valuables. Another boat draws alongside, and its occupant addresses Gaffer Hexam as 'pardner', a title which Gaffer is quick to repudiate. Lizzie rows for home; the dreadful thing attached to Gaffer's boat 'followed submissively'.

The Cup and the Lip The title of Book 1 is the second part of a proverbial saying, which begins 'There's many a slip twixt . . .'. This and the subsequent Book headings, which are also proverbial 'halves', are very much a part of the symmetrical structure of the novel.

London Bridge which is of stone Opened in 1831; Southwark (of iron) was opened in 1819.

lighterman i.e. plying his boat to take off the load of a larger boat which could not be unloaded at the wharf.

a muffled human form River-finders or dredgers searched the Thames for bodies, always confident of finding either money or turning the discovery to good account at the inquest.

bird of prey The image associated with the trade, but also a central image in terms of chapter headings and structure in the novel.

I cannot sit so near it The first positive indication of Lizzie's moral function in the novel.

Gaffer Master, old man.

wulturs i.e. vultures (note the immediate bird of prey associations).

Has a dead man any use for money Note the series of rhetorical questions.

stretcher The board in the boat against which the rower presses his feet.

the high moralities The very reverse – he has bluntly asserted what he will do.

neophyte Beginner, novice, new convert; again ironic.

Chapter 2 The Man From Somewhere

This chapter is in complete contrast to the first, though it involves another introduction, this time to those 'bran-new' people the Veneerings – the name is particularly revealing. Twemlow, the character around whom their initial society hospitality is built, is compared to an article of furniture, a comparison later seen to be appropriate when his lack of animation is established. He is bewildered by his own position. Then a Veneering 'banquet' is described, with the comedy of Podsnap mistaking Twemlow for his host. Podsnap's 'fatal freshness' is given a considered stress. This chapter is a finely satirical account of the insincerities and hypocrisies of fashionable society; at the centre is a mirror reflection of that society, the mirror in a sense conveying the essential egocentricity. The irony is delicious throughout (note especially the portrait of Lady Tippins), but there are some important plot clues laid regarding John Harmon, who is mentioned by Mortimer Lightwood to Eugene Wrayburn. The dust empire is also described, with an account of the girl who has to marry the man chosen for her – he is the inheritor of the 'Mounds', which themselves symbolize a form of riches. Dramatic tension rises, for Mortimer reveals that the man is on the way home – and, at the end of the chapter, that he has been found drowned.

Veneering Note the name (and all other Dickens names), which exactly suggests the *superficiality* of the characters.

Pantechnicon Furniture warehouse, originally the name of a bazaar.

take soundings of i.e. make calculations, estimate.

excogitation Thinking out, resolution of.

a Member, an Engineer The whole list is simply personified to indicate the public or specialized importance of these particular social climbers – or those who will assist the Veneerings to climb.

fatal freshness Sarcastic reference to Podsnap's self-satisfied insincere brand of 'charm'.

Antinous A youth renowned for his beauty, favourite of the Emperor Hadrian. He drowned himself in the Nile in AD 130.

feeble might But Twemlow grows in stature, and is in some ways one of the moral yardsticks of the novel. Completely negative here (perhaps *Twemlow* = *tremulous*) he later becomes possessed of right feelings with regard to the marriage of Eugene Wrayburn and Lizzie Hexam.

ye unhappy children of men Dickens is very fond of Biblical, prayer, or hymn parody, and this is a good example.

Court Circular Daily report of the doings of the Royal Family published in the newspapers.

a remunerative article i.e. one to be cultivated, worth knowing because of his aristocratic connections.

Analytical Chemist To the disillusioned retainer, all things connected with society life merit close examination and distrust – even the wine.

Chablis Dry white wine of Burgundy.

The Herald's College The body existing to trace genealogies and to grant coats-of-arms; founded in 1483, and presided over by the Dukes of Norfolk.

Professor Owen A scathing reference to Mrs Podsnap's unattractive features. Professor Sir Richard Owen (1804–92) was a famous anatomist with a special interest in fossil mammals and birds.

First-Gentleman-in-Europe A reference to George IV (1762–1830), so referred to for his style and manners.

Like a face in a tablespoon . . . Long Walk Note just how ridiculous the author is making someone who sets great store by her own appearance and effect.

this hardy old cruiser has last touched Note the satirical tone – yet the image is related to the 'boats' of the story.

Cymon From Dryden's 'Cymon and Iphigenia from Boccace'; one of Dryden's *Fables* (1700) taken from the *Decameron of Boccaccio*. Cymon was a good-looking but dull and degenerate young man: 'And Cymon call'd which signifies a brute; So well his name did with his nature sute'. Banished by his father he fell in love with Iphigenia and returned after many trials, transformed by his love for her. Lady Tippins hopes her fictitious lover, too, will turn out well in the end.

like the legs of scratching poultry Malicious description of Lady Tippins's ageing neck, making the stories about her lovers even more incongruous.

Cupidon Cupid was the boy god of Love. Lady Tippins is referring to her 'list'.

Tease! Pay! The affectations of Lady Tippins are taken up by Mrs Veneering – here meaning 'Please! Pray! (or Play!)'.

local habitation A phrase from *A Midsummer Night's Dream* Act 5, Scene 1: 'A local habitation and name'. It is part of the Dickensian irony here not to complete the quotation.

Day and Martin's Slang at that time for a Negro, because this brand of blacking was particularly black – a typical piece of Wrayburn flippancy.

Cape Wine Wine from that province in South Africa.

Made his money by Dust i.e. by selling the dust, which would be domestic refuse collected by private Contractors.

that popular character ... versifiers call Another Dickens cannot resist an occasional jibe at his fellow novelists.

screw it slowly into themselves Note the turn of phrase: inward instead of outward movement.

Madeira Wine from this island in the Atlantic Ocean.

Don Juan The legendary lover, subject of a poem by Lord Byron (1788–1824); but Lady Tippins – with lovers her first waking thought – is addressing Mortimer.

Commendatore Lady Tippins continues the Don Juan image by referring to the Analytical Chemist as 'the Commendatore', the old man killed in a duel by Don Giovanni in Mozart's opera (1787).

Chapter 3 Another Man

It is Hexam's son, a boy of fifteen, who has brought the message, and Eugene and Mortimer set out with the boy. Mortimer is a solicitor, Eugene a barrister, both barely employed and not exactly in love with their jobs. The boy takes them to an area that is both land and water. They arrive at his home, and Gaffer reveals to his visitors the placards in his possession; at that moment a stranger, who is lost, appears. They all go to the police station. The Night Inspector shows them a body, which has been identified. The stranger is obviously upset by all this but, at the Inspector's request, writes down his name and address.

Gaffer goes off to the public house, and Charley returns to his sister Lizzie. She reminds him of the pictures she has seen in the fire, and also talks about their past life together when she was both sister and mother to him. To his delight, she looks into the future: she sees him acquiring education; but because of this he will be separated from her father and herself. Next day Jesse Hexam appears as a witness at the Six Jolly Fellowship Porters before a Coroner's jury; the deceased is recorded as being Mr John Harmon, while the motive for his death is thought to have been robbery. A reward is offered for information; and the Night Inspector ponders the case, which is initially much talked of, then fades from the public consciousness.

going to Canterbury in more gold frame i.e. the picture was overshadowed by the heavy ornate gilt frame.

a plait i.e. a 'pleat'; a flattened fold in the cloth.

Pharoah's multitude ... in the Red Sea ... only half as far gone The first reference is to Exodus 14, the second to John 11.

Cassim Baba, in the robber's cave The brother of Ali Baba of *Ali Baba and the Forty Thieves* fame.

the Monument ... the Tower ... the Docks ... Ratcliffe See the section on *Background and foreground*.

a rotten wart of wood upon its forehead The personification is important, for Dickens often makes buildings reflect their inhabitants or associations.

shaped like a hyacinth-root Again note the fertility of the imaginative association.

list Edge of cloth, selvage.

I'm scholar enough There is a terrible irony in this, in view of what his education does for him, and what formal education does for his son Charley.

his ruffled crest stood highest Part of the bird sequence of imagery that stresses the predatory nature of Hexam.

as if he were in a monastery on top of a mountain The image, at first sight odd, conveys the isolated nature of police work.

illuminating a missal Decorating the initial letters in a Roman Catholic service book in gold, silver or brilliant colours.

A bull's-eye . . . satellite A kind of lantern provided by one of his subordinates.

Reserve A trained policeman, but not one on the beat.

wanted 'prenticeship i.e. needed training for.

Stomach and not Mind i.e. he had a weak stomach, rather than being emotional.

Pupil-teacher This system began in 1846. The pupil-teachers were instructed in their duties by the head-teacher of the school.

behoof Advantage.

Chapter 4 The R. Wilfer Family

This chapter opens with a description of R. Wilfer: 'a poor clerk' of cherubic appearance and very shy, he works in the drug house that has Veneering as its main partner. We first meet him going home to Holloway, and there the eccentricities of Mrs Wilfer are described; we also meet Bella. Husband and wife argue a little over the letting of a room, and at one stage Bella wilfully sweeps the draughts and the board on to the floor. We further learn that Bella is bereaved, for she is the girl who was to have married John Harmon, though she had never met him. Bella deplores her poverty, and also the fact that the Harmon murder is the talk of the town. Shortly after this, the stranger who is to have the room arrives. He signs his name as John Rokesmith; Bella takes, or affects to take, a dislike to him; the situation is saved by R. Wilfer standing treat for the family. Bella makes a great fuss of her father and argues with her sister Lavinia (Lavvy), while the last lines of the chapter reveal to the reader that Julius Handford and John Rokesmith are one and the same man.

the Conqueror i.e. William the Conqueror, in 1066.
pantaloons Trousers or breeches and stockings in one piece.
conventional Cherub i.e. plump innocence depicted in paintings.
when he was not put down i.e. not put rigorously in his place.
drug-markets Remember that Chicksey, Veneering and Company dealt in drugs for medicines.
peg-top A reference to a child's wooden spinning-top.
suburban Sahara The latter is the great Libyan desert, an apt image, in view of the Dust Mounds which are to be described.
the huffing ... the coronation of an opponent In draughts, the penalty for failing to take another piece, and the making up of a piece into a king after it has reached an opponent's end square.
orange chips Slices of orange peel prepared for eating.
Old Master A painting by one of the great artists of the past.
something will come of it Prophetic words, though not in the way that Bella means them – for ultimately what comes of it is that she marries 'Rokesmith'.
the viand i.e. the veal-cutlet.
a dowdy little puss i.e. a drab young woman.
Rokesmith was the man Note that the author is laying heavy clues in his own plot at this early point.

Chapter 5 Boffin's Bower

The chapter opens with a fine description of Silas Wegg, his occupation and his 'post' near Cavendish Square being defined. Wegg has adopted in his imagination (and there is something pathetic in this) the inmates of a house outside which he has his stall. Wegg is approached by Mr Boffin, who reveals after some discussion that he is in need of a reader for the evenings. After negotiations with the unscrupulous Wegg, Boffin agrees that the latter shall come to him and read, Wegg finds his way with difficulty to Boffin's Bower, meets Mrs Boffin and undertakes the reading – having eaten a large pie which he has noticed. We suspect that Wegg is out for what he can make.

water-cart i.e. carrying water for damping down the roads.
'Out House' Although Wegg is an undesirable character, there is a certain pathetic quality in his wishing to associate himself with what is really family life, though it is far removed from him.
Magna Charta This reference to the acceptance by King John in 1215 of the supremacy of the law over the will of the monarch is here intended to imply that the measure gave an unimpeachable value of nuts.
the Quality i.e. gentry.
alphabeds ... wollumes Obviously 'alphabets' and 'volumes' – but Wegg has many odd pronunciations, just like the eccentric notice he displays.
Fair Rosamond's Henry II was said to have hidden his mistress Rosamond in a house in Woodstock where no one could find her without detailed instruction.
a speeches of chaff Probably 'species', perhaps given to blowing about, hence subject to many moods.
apotheosis i.e. release from earthly life.
a highflyer at Fashion i.e. keeps up with the latest fashion or vogue.
tap-room For the selling and drinking of beer, spirits etc.
continny i.e. continue.

Canine Provision Trade Presumably dog meat and biscuits or meal.

the organ moist The throat lubricated.

mellers it i.e. mellows it.

mixing i.e. a drink.

The Decline and Fall of the Roman Empire By Edward Gibbon (1737–94), who dedicated his life to writing it. The first volume was published in 1776, the last in 1788. The names mentioned by Dickens – 'Hadrian', 'Trajan' and 'the Antonines' – occur on the first page of Gibbon's first chapter, and all fall in the period (AD 98–180). Commodus is killed near the end of Chapter 4 of the *Decline and Fall* (in AD 192), which leads one to believe that Silas's first reading is something of a marathon.

Vittle-us Vitellius (AD 15–69), Roman Emperor referred to in Chapter 3 of *The Decline and Fall of the Roman Empire* as 'the beastly Vitellius', with a footnote explaining that he 'gave himself up to excessive gluttony and other vices'.

scarers i.e. frightening events and examples.

Chapter 6 Cut Adrift

After the eccentric Wegg and the eccentric Boffin, a description of the eccentric Six Jolly Fellowship Porters. The scene opens with Miss Abbey Potterson upbraiding Rogue Riderhood, who is intent on damning his ex-'pardner' Gaffer Hexam. He asserts that Gaffer makes a habit of attacking people, pushing them into the river, then picking up their bodies. He threatens to expose Gaffer, however long it takes. Miss Abbey evinces a personal interest in her customers, telling each one when he has to leave. She summons Lizzie to her, acquaints her with the suspicions against her father, and tries to persuade Lizzie to leave him. She then bans Gaffer from the house. Lizzie goes home and determines that her brother Charley shall have his chance. Charley wakes, is in two minds about leaving, but in the end lets his sister have her way. After his departure Lizzie waits for her father, and the latter disowns the son who has left him. Lizzie is frightened by her father's anger and the knife in his hand, but he displays great tenderness towards her.

riven Split.
you might trace little forests there An imaginative sequence, comparable in its effect to Lizzie and Charley looking into the fire.
sugar-loaf hats Steeple-crowned hats, as worn by witches and Welsh women in the seventeenth to nineteenth centuries.
purl Hot beer with a glass of gin in it.
Flip Hot beer and brandy spiced and sweetened.
Dog's Nose Gin and beer mixed.
in Quod i.e. in prison.
criminate i.e. incriminate, condemn yourself.
purwiding Providing.
Port Negus Hot sweetened port wine and water.
so rattled to bed i.e. sent to bed sharply and roughly.
And as the great black river The description is prophetic of the dark deeds to come.
The white face of the winter day came sluggishly on Note the fine personification of this paragraph, which symbolically suggests Lizzie's suffering, the quality of her imagination and the mixture of events that will characterize her life.
She saw that the mute avoidance had begun One realizes that Gaffer is sensitive to his daughter's abhorrence of his 'trade'.
Have we got a pest in the house Note the ominous associations of this, almost as if Gaffer is doomed – as indeed he is.

Chapter 7 Mr Wegg looks after himself

Silas Wegg pays a visit to Mr Venus, a preserver of animals and birds. Mr Venus invites Wegg to partake of tea and muffins, and Silas never refuses. Mr Venus 'articulates' human bones; and he is much oppressed by being unhappily in love. He provides Wegg with information about the

Boffins, asking if there is any truth in the rumour that Mr Boffin has hidden anything of value in the Mounds. Wegg thinks not, but a seed has been sown in his devious mind.

for Nature has already screwed both pretty tight The image, though grotesque, is typical of Wegg, who later does his utmost to screw everything that he can out of Mr Boffin.

dealers in dogs and singing-birds The interested reader will refer to Mayhew's mammoth *Life and Labour of the London Poor*, which obviously influenced Dickens, and which indicates so many of the occupations of Londoners at the time.

two preserved frogs fighting a small-sword duel Stephen Gill points out that Forster in his *Life of Dickens* refers to just such a pair of ornaments on Dickens's own writing-desk.

Mr Venus Based on an original trader with the more commonplace name of Willis.

Cock Robin, the hero of the ballad 'Who Killed Cock Robin?', the well-known children's rhyme. But note that Wegg often introduces his own variations on ballad, song and poetic themes; remember too that he sells ballads, so this is an appropriate reference.

articulating i.e. connecting the joints.

to collect myself like a genteel person Wegg meant 'kept in one piece'.

Potentate A monarch or ruler.

that port Note the sea image, a constant in this novel.

Chapter 8 Mr Boffin in Consultation

Mr Boffin visits the offices of Mortimer Lightwood, where he is received by young Blight. His name is entered in the Callers' Book, the clerk keeping up the pretence that his employer has a large number of clients. Mortimer arrives and confirms the magnitude of the Boffin inheritance since the death of John Harmon. Mr Boffin recalls his own experiences with his employer, and gives a graphic description of his last meeting with the seven-year-old John Harmon prior to his being packed off to 'that foreign school'. Following some more talk about the inheritance, Mr Boffin arranges for Mortimer to draw up a will leaving his entire estate to Mrs Boffin. Eugene Wrayburn arrives, in flippant mood. Mr Boffin leaves and is tracked down Fleet Street by John Rokesmith, who says he would like to become Mr Boffin's Secretary and reveals that he is lodging with the Wilfers. Strangely, Bella's name has been in Mr Boffin's mind all morning, and for some days before.

Pertinax Dickens keeps to the sequence of *The Decline and Fall of The Roman Empire*. This is still in the first volume, the Emperor's career being described after the death of Commodus (AD 161–192). Pertinax ruled for only three months, in AD 193.
praetorian guards The bodyguards of a Roman general or Emperor.
Familiar Spirit A spirit slave in human or animal form – supposedly a witch's demon in disguise.
blue bag i.e. one containing a barrister's papers.
parboiled i.e. overheated, hotly involved with. (The correct, culinary, meaning is 'partly boiled' before final roasting or frying.)
Rocky Mountains Western North American range.
Tartar Native of Tartary, group including Cossacks, hence savage.
sarser Saucer.
a rattler i.e. a good strong blow.
a country contract ... sifted before carted i.e. which was to be roughly examined, to see what it contained, before being loaded up and taken away.
Doctors' Commons Where a number of the Courts of Law were held; Dickens himself was employed there for a time.
a whole tool-box of edged tools Mortimer is saying that there will be many temptations (i.e. towards perjury and false information) because of the size of the reward.
Tuft-hunting Seeking the society of titled or otherwise prominent people.

mantling i.e. blood suffusing the cheeks, blushing.
plump it out i.e. speak bluntly.
cat-preserve i.e. small area haunted by cats.

Chapter 9 Mr and Mrs Boffin in Consultation

The Boffins discuss their situation, Mrs Boffin announcing with a good deal of pleasure that she wants 'Society'. She also needs someone to look after the Bower, and she would like to have Bella to live with them. Her particular wish is to adopt an orphan to take the place of little John Harmon, who never returned. The old couple are honest, and were obviously respected by their employer. They decide to call upon Bella, but first visit the Reverend Frank Milvey to discuss the possibility of adopting an orphan. Mr Boffin then asked Mr Milvey to 'do him the kindness to be perpetually his banker to the extent of a twenty-pound note or so, to be expended without any reference to him'. The Boffins then visit the Wilfers, with something of a pantomime before they are admitted, and the proposition is made to Bella (with Lavinia loudly voicing her objections). When the Boffins finally withdraw, they meet John Rokesmith. The histrionic Mrs Wilfer pronounces Mrs Boffin 'cunning'.

like Wax-Work Madame Tussaud came to London in 1802 and began her display of wax-work dummies of the famous and infamous.
Lor-a-mussy Lord have mercy.
poled Rammed by the centre pole or one of the shafts of the vehicle behind.
Evil often stops short at itself . . . Good, never This is a clear moral commentary on the theme of the novel.
hammer-headed Stupid, obstinate.
her want of i.e. her desire for.

blankets . . . being turned into liquor i.e. whatever we provided (as payment) would be sold to provide them with drink.
brisk her up i.e. give her a lively time.

Chapter 10 A Marriage Contract

We return to the Veneerings, and this provides an opportunity for the author to attack the nature of high finance and share-speculation. Twemlow is invited to dinner (with Podsnap), and it is agreed that he will give away the bride in the forthcoming society wedding. The preparations begin, and old Lady Tippins starts 'to be dyed and varnished for the interesting occasion'. The reception breakfast is given a like satirical slant, and the humour takes a somewhat different turn when the 'Analytical' has his dignity hit by a heavy shoe cast after the bride and bridegroom as they set off for the Isle of Wight. Then there is a switch to the already inharmoniously-paired honeymoon couple – it turns out that each, thinking to have married money and property, has in fact married poverty. Each has been misled about the other by Veneering. They are both mortified, but agree to keep their secret, with Alfred Lammle the dominating character.

traffic in Shares It has been rightly noted that the 1860s saw many crashes on the stock market. Veneering is to suffer much later, but Lammle is a fake.
henbane A poisonous herb of the nightshade family.
Relieve us of our money Again this rhetoric is linked to the theme of the novel and it is enhanced here by the biblical tone of the language.
Hymen In Greek mythology, the god of marriage.
Colossus at Rhodes The magnificent statue of Apollo, one of the wonders of the Ancient World, which reputedly stood 120 ft high astride the harbour at Rhodes. By comparison Podsnap is indeed a 'statuette'.

Stucconia Dickens's own ironic coinage, since stucco is a kind of cement or plaster used for covering the (often defective) outside walls of buildings. Hence the associations are with the artificial, not the real, just as in the case of the name Veneering.

curacoa Liqueur of spirits flavoured with the peel of bitter oranges.

like adorable recruits . . . a barrack of strangers Not infrequently there are little flurries of images like this, which form a sequence.

galvanic starts Twitching, even jumping, in sleep.

King George the Third (1728–1820); suffering from insanity during the last thirty years of his life.

Mephistophiles (Nowadays generally spelt 'Mephistopheles'.) The impersonation of the devil in Goethe's *Faust*.

Medusa One of the three Gorgons who, in Greek mythology, had the power of turning into stone anyone who looked at them.

petrifaction i.e. paralysis caused by terror.

oilcake-fed Mass of compressed linseed used as cattle fodder.

scarlatina Scarlet fever.

ottomans Cushioned seats like sofas but without back or arms; a type of divan.

the face i.e. the nerve.

like white steps . . . the diabolical performer A superb image and association, redolent of evil.

twitting me Making fun of me, mocking me.

A devil of a temper A further underlining of the Mephistophelean qualities of Alfred Lammle.

Chapter 11 Podsnappery

Here Mr Podsnap's self-satisfaction is described; and his determination to let nothing encroach upon that self-satisfaction (achieved by brushing aside all problems, and burying his head firmly in the sand). His daughter Miss Podsnap has a tendency to blush – as we see from the account of the entertainment for Georgiana's eighteenth birthday. Podsnap's condescension, to the French gentleman in particular, is dwelt on, and there is also an account of his blinkered and misguided patriotism. Details of the Harmon affair are produced by the Veneerings; and Mrs Veneering has seen Bella. The Podsnap 'mutton vapour-bath' and 'bathers' are described. Mrs Lammle deliberately makes up to poor Miss Podsnap, who has little conversation and many nerves. She is, however, carried off to the 'sets', first by 'the Ogre' Mr Grompus and then by the man with 'a glass in his eye'. Podsnap, confronted with the report that people are starving in the streets, refuses to acknowledge that there is any truth in it; later he puts everything down to Providence. Podsnap finishes the evening in undisturbed complacency, while Lammle urges his wife: 'Keep close to that idiot girl.'

Marine Insurance The insurance of ships against loss.
PRESTO Quickly, rapidly (normally used by conjurers).
rocking-horse ... art of prancing Note the image, which indicates the artificial nature of the exercise and not the natural reality.
tooled Drove.
custard-coloured phaeton Light four-wheeled open carriage. Note the colour, which conveys the ostentation of the proceeding.
friends of their souls Note the hyperbole, which accurately captures the society's tone.
to bespeak a well-conducted automaton i.e. to hire a dance conductor for the evening.
a mushroom man i.e. one who was rising, coming up in the world.
A corpulent straddling epergne A large and ostentatious centre ornament for the dinner table.
'ma fille' My daughter.
énormément Enormously.
Mais, yees Why, yes.
ESKER *Est-ce que?*: the sum-total of the sallowish gentleman's knowledge of French.
Mais oui ... Quoi donc Why, certainly ... What is it?

Pavvy Mr Podsnap's incompetent attempt to say *pavé* ('pavement').
alwiz Always.
ozer Other.
legatee i.e. who has been left the money.
like partners at cards who played a game against All England Splendid image to underline the fact that the Lammles must gamble to survive.
take a rock Part of the rocking-horse image.
if I had been a chimney sweep on May-day A marvellous imaginative leap which takes her out of the artificial society and into the world of the deprived but living. May-day marked the beginning of a season of constant work for the chimney sweep – cause enough for celebration.
frumpy Old-fashioned, dowdily dressed.
Terpsichorean art i.e. dancing, from Terpsichore, the muse of dancing.
Utopian From the *Utopia* of Sir Thomas More, the prose account of the imaginary island with the perfect political organization.
presentation-curtesys i.e. when, for example, presenting a bouquet.
the Ogre . . . castle in the top couple This is the figure of the dance, but the image reflects the childlike qualities of Georgiana, and makes her role in society the more pathetic.
a nutmeg . . . coloured warm water i.e. spiced wine, but the implication (as with the 'mutton vapour-bath') is that the Podsnaps are mean.

Chapter 12 The Sweat of an Honest Man's Brow

Lightwood and Wrayburn take dinner together in Lightwood's office. Wrayburn wryly contemplates his position as an (unemployed) barrister, which had been arbitrarily laid down for him by his father. A 'ghost' in the shape of Rogue Riderhood, who wishes to swear an affidavit, knocks at the door; he has, in fact, come to lay information to the effect that Gaffer Hexam killed John Harmon. Lightwood tells him that this is merely Riderhood's suspicion; but Riderhood insists that Hexam had told him that he did it. Riderhood then takes them to the Six Jolly Fellowship Porters, and on to the police station. The Inspector returns to the public house with Lightwood and Wrayburn.

Thomson's Seasons (1700–48). *The Seasons* was published 1726–30, and ran into a number of editions.
top-sawyers i.e. employed in sawing wood, but having better jobs than the bottom or under-sawyers.
the sparrows repented . . . like men and women The sentence is ironic, and has particular reference to the Lammles.
Circuit i.e. Courts held in particular districts, to which barristers must travel.
Wallsend Coal from that area of Northumberland; he wanted to talk by the glow of firelight.
Circumnavigator i.e. one who sails round.
'tickler business' i.e. particular business.
Alfred David Riderhood's version of 'affidavit', a written statement confirmed by oath, to be used as judicial proof.
drowned dog, or cat i.e. the sodden cap.
took down i.e. you must write the statement.
summa't Something.
Of seaman's pocket i.e. of stealing.
cause'ays i.e. causeways.
he's fell off from i.e. that people are shunning him (because of their suspicions).
Draggin i.e. dragon.
Hages i.e. ages, for a long time.
that as turned me i.e. that which made me choose to tell.
And echo answered Eugene is being sarcastic; this is a reference to Byron's poem 'The Corsair' (1814): 'Where is my child?' – An echo answers – 'Where?'
again i.e. against.
cut-throat Shepherds i.e. they will betray those they are watching.
The honest man Note the quiet irony of the phrase.

coolly tossed it under the grate Note the contempt in the action.
in his stock i.e. the high-neckcloth he was wearing.
reckoned up i.e. calculated his misdeeds.
in it . . . spotted Collaborating . . . accused.
Northfleet Kentish town on the north bank of the Thames estuary, near Gravesend.
lime The word is used as a cover and, by analogy, to define the relationship between Riderhood and Gaffer Hexam.

Chapter 13 Tracking the Bird of Prey

The three men establish themselves in the Cosy, and they learn that Lizzie is at home waiting for Hexam to return. Riderhood reports that he has not yet come back. Eugene goes alone to watch Lizzie as she waits. He stands unseen at her window, and sees her sitting in the firelight weeping. Suddenly she opens the door and calls her father. Eugene, restless, returns to the Cosy. All three now await the arrival of Gaffer. Rogue Riderhood goes in search of him, but finds the boat empty.

a mouthful of fire i.e. a coal fire in the grate.
burn sherry i.e. mull it.
Guy Fawkes The conspirator who attempted to blow up the Houses of Parliament in 1605.
myrmidons Hired ruffians (originating from the warlike Thessalian people who followed Achilles). But here Eugene is doubtless referring to policemen.
Gulliver with the Lilliputians firing upon him *Gulliver's Travels*, by Dean Swift (1667–1745), was published in 1726, and as a child Dickens read it constantly. The reference here is to Chapter 1 of *Gulliver*.
and extinguish him i.e. put out the flame of life.
thowels Thole pins, the oar being inserted in them to provide leverage.

Chapter 14 The Bird of Prey Brought Down

Riderhood has tied up Gaffer's boat and they use his own for the search, but they have to face a sudden squall. Riderhood then leads them to Hexam's abandoned boat, from which there is a rope trailing over the side. They bring the boat to land, haul the rope in and find Gaffer's body attached to the end. The Inspector unties the rope and explains that death came about accidentally, through Gaffer's going overboard and inadvertently tightening the short rope about his neck. Eugene disappears; Mortimer goes home, exhausted by the events of the night; and Eugene turns up in Mortimer's rooms the following afternoon.

like inscriptions over the graves of dead businesses Eugene has a prophetic imagination, which takes in the large and the small: the bringing down of Gaffer and, later, of Fledgeby and Veneering.

Figure-head i.e. under the bowsprit of a ship.

Wolf in bed in Grandmamma's cottage Dickens is referring to Little Red Riding Hood, undoubtedly by association with Rogue Riderhood, who is certainly a wolf.

M.R.F. My respected father, earlier referred to as a title like that of the Duke of Wellington.

somnambulist Sleepwalker.

the Newgate Calendar Originally published in the 1770s as an account of leading criminals. It was re-issued during the nineteenth century and exercised a great influence on Dickens and his contemporaries.

Chapter 15 Two New Servants

A return to the Boffins. Rokesmith arrives, demonstrates his efficiency as a Secretary and is taken on – largely at the instigation of Mrs Boffin. Boffin reveals that they have bought a new home and he also warns Rokesmith that he must not arouse the jealousy of Silas Wegg. There follows a description of the Bower, or Harmony Jail. The Secretary is shown around and made aware of the Boffins' kindness. They intend to keep up the house, but to sell the Mounds. Later, in order to enable Wegg to give up his stall, Boffin offers to buy him out – he wants him to look after the Bower when they move. Mrs Boffin disturbs their declining-and-falling by her feeling that the past is still with them, that the house is haunted. Wegg is sent home and the Boffins take a walk.

stertorous Making snoring sounds.

a Secretary to be a piece of furniture The confusion is with the French *secrétaire*, which is an escritoire or writing-desk.

Steward i.e. a person entrusted with the management of property, but Mr Boffin associates the word with a *ship's* steward.

Apple-pie order In an immaculately tidy condition.

iron-moulding your linen Mrs Boffin knows that unless her husband employs a Secretary to write his letters for him, his shirts will permanently carry the brown stain left by ink.

neck and crop i.e. completely.

A gloomy house the Bower It should, of course, be the reverse in view of its name. Harmony and Jail are equally paradoxical.

desuetude Having passed into a state of disuse.

low cunning ... high simplicity Each is the antithesis of the other – and at first it looks as if Wegg will succeed.

Belisarius (AD 505–65) The Byzantine general of the Emperor Justinian; he is mentioned in Volume 4 of *The Decline and Fall* – an indication of the area covered so far by Wegg's reading.

Thrown on the wide world A verse from a ballad with music by John Parry.

Weep for the hour From *Eveleen's Bower*, one of the Irish ballads of Thomas Moore (1779–1852).

we will call clover i.e. the best, the ideal.

Then farewell my trim-built wherry Wegg quoting again, this time from *The Waterman*, by Charles Dibden (1745–1814).

Bully Sawyers ... impending expedition against the Persians Some twenty pages on in the fourth volume of *The Decline and Fall* after the mention of Belisarius.

Chapter 16 Minders and Re-minders

Mortimer Lightwood is looking for Julius Handford, and arranges for an advertisement to be inserted daily in all the newspapers for six weeks. There is then a description of the 'bargain' and 'sale' of orphans; eventually Rokesmith and Mrs Boffin go to Brentford to see Betty Higden, and are introduced to Sloppy. There follows an indictment by Betty Higden (and Charles Dickens) of the Poor Law; Sloppy is further examined. Betty breaks down when Mrs Boffin talks of taking Johnny, the orphan she is nursing at the moment. They talk, Betty's independence of the Poor Law being stressed. Later Rokesmith goes for a walk and meets Bella. He tells her that he is now Mr Boffin's Secretary, and that Mrs Boffin will be ready to receive her within a week. Mrs Wilfer joins them, refers patronizingly to Bella's forthcoming move to the Boffins, and Rokesmith retires, thinking how mercenary – and how pretty – Bella is.

swearing your way through a stone wall i.e. against anything.

I don't think it promises i.e. I don't think that it will achieve anything.

rigged i.e. falsified.

scrip Provisional certificate later entitling the holder to dividends.

a gallon of beer i.e. a bargaining price.

a wild and South-Sea nature A reference to the financial crisis known as the South Sea Bubble in 1720.

a small home with a large mangle In seven words Dickens describes Betty Higden's poverty, her cleanliness and the heavy work demanded of her over the years of caring for her young charges.

scarlet-beans . . . Fates were propitious Runner-beans . . . if the weather was right.

hearts may count in Heaven as high as heads i.e. goodness of heart on earth may be valued more highly than rank.

He do the Police in different voices Interestingly, the phrase was used as a heading by T. S. Eliot in Part 1 of *The Waste Land*, but later deleted. Sloppy is a good mimic and later proves himself to be something of an actor, an attribute he shares with John Harmon.

The Poor-house ... a corpse of us there Stephen Gill refers to Mayhew and to Charles Reade (a contemporary of Dickens) for possible sources of Betty and her rejection of the Poor Law.

put off i.e. turned away.

Union money i.e. provided from the funds of a group of parishes.

She paid scot and she paid lot She had no debts; she paid immediately.

ricketty i.e. suffering from rickets: softening of the bones, bow-legged.

investing it in wrong securities i.e. not able to act in a fully controlled way; note that the image is once again of high finance.

Still with that light beat upon her hard rough hand Indicative of her emotional heart-beat: her concern for her children past and present.

trumped the trick i.e. went one better.

inveigled Craftily persuaded.

richly-caparisoned i.e. finely-equipped.

Lavater Johann Kaspar Lavater (1741–1801), Swiss Protestant and writer. His great work on physiognomy (the art of judging character from features of face or form of body) was *Physiognomische Fragmente zur Beförderung der Menschenkenntniss und Menschenliebe* (*1775–8*).

luminous elucidation i.e. clear definition – heavy sarcasm on the part of the author.

And if she knew i.e. if she realized that he was John Harmon.

like a Ghost Appropriate comment; when Lightwood, Potterson and Kibble later see John they are sure that they *are* seeing one.

Chapter 17 A Dismal Swamp

The parasites surround the Boffins, from individuals to what Dickens calls the 'corporate beggars'; the various types of begging letters and tricks of the trade are described. Silas Wegg (perhaps the greatest parasite of all) is established in the house and embarks on his own secret and somewhat sinister exploration of the many nooks and crannies.

One copper-plate ... two copper-plates i.e. visiting-cards left at the houses of newcomers to a district. In accordance with the social custom Mrs Veneering leaves one card for Mrs Boffin and Mr Veneering leaves two: one for Mr Boffin and one for both Mr and Mrs Boffin.

taking the air in a mutton grove i.e. a butcher's shop.

marked by a stroke of notoriety i.e. who has inherited or won a large sum of money (today's winners of football pools frequently receive begging letters).

the Peninsula A reference to the Peninsular War (1808–14) fought in Spain and Portugal between the French on the one hand and the Spanish, Portuguese and British (under Wellington) on the other.

There are beggars on horseback too The proverb is generally taken as 'Set a beggar on horseback and he'll ride to the Devil' (but there are variants, such as: 'If wishes were horses, beggars would ride').

sporting ventures i.e. gambling, taking a chance.

Book 2 Birds of a Feather

Chapter 1 Of an Educational Character

Charley Hexam is at school in a loft. Dickens gives a satirical account of the ludicrously unsuitable choice of books for the very young. The lack of comprehension and the inevitable weariness of the pupils is also described. At Charley's wish he and Bradley Headstone visit his sister Lizzie, and Miss Peecher, the schoolmistress next door, and her assistant watch them depart. Charley and Headstone arrive at the 'Doll's Dressmaker's'. When she appears it is obvious that the schoolmaster is interested in her. They go for a walk by the river, Headstone sauntering on while Charley and Lizzie talk. Charley reveals that he is ashamed of Lizzie, and afraid that she will 'pull him back' in his attempts to better himself. After they part, Eugene Wrayburn strolls past them and is recognized by Charley. Bradley discusses the possibility of his marrying Lizzie at some later date, should she prove suitable.

The school A reference to one of the Ragged schools, which Dickens deplored.
nankeen Kind of cotton cloth (from Nanking, China).
mudlarks Street arabs, urchins.
supernatural possession ... shining light Dickens is mocking the simple Christian story with a moral about the poor, which has no resemblance to reality.
prosiest Dullest.
chief executioner The tone underlines Dickens's irony.
acolyte Assistant, novice.
blinkers i.e. worn by a horse so that it was not distracted by what was happening on either side.
Sepulchre Dickens is satirizing the form of pedantry that utters long words without defining them.
High Market i.e. an important market in a large (country) town.

highly certificated stipendiary schoolmaster Again the ironic tone is evident. Provision was made for the training of teachers in 1846, and those first to qualify were teaching by 1853.

take her in the rough i.e. accept her as you find her.

mechanical stowage i.e. storing what he learned, committing it to memory. Note the link with 'mental warehouse' and 'stock' that follow.

to be told off for i.e. destined for, pushed towards that career.

The schools Stephen Gill believes them to be in Deptford.

the locomotive gift of Aladdin's palace Further reference to *The Arabian Nights*: at a rub of the magic lamp the palace was instantly transported to the farthest corner of Africa – a further rub just as swiftly returned it.

like a toy neighbourhood ... set up anyhow This again is a criticism of government and the establishment, for the implication is that the planning is very poor.

frowziness Unkempt, neglected, dingy.

a Jack's beanstalk A reference to the famous beanstalk in the fairy tale which grew to an enormous height overnight.

took a refresher i.e. learned again.

Like the Miller of questionable jollity in the song The reference is to 'The Miller of Dee': 'I care for nobody, no, not I/And nobody cares for me.'

Pen-wipers Small pieces of cloth for wiping pens after use.

forfeits Jenny goes on to play this particular guessing game with its penalties.

Bedlam Properly, Bethlem Hospital, formerly the hospital of St Mary of Bethlehem, for the insane.

a Doll's Dressmaker i.e. making clothes for dolls for children whose rich parents could afford them.

bills Placards, indicating wanted people, criminals, etc.

mooning about i.e. doing nothing in particular.

N.B. *Nota bene* (Latin: 'mark well').

Chapter 2 Still Educational

Lizzie returns to the doll's dressmaker's. The name of the latter is Fanny Cleaver, but she has chosen to dispense with this, and calls herself Jenny Wren. She is a happy and lively soul despite her deformity. Then Eugene Wrayburn calls; he has previously offered to teach Lizzie – and Jenny – and thus to give her the education she had wished for her brother. Lizzie finally agrees, and Jenny talks of small flowers and of her dreams as a child. Then Jenny's own 'child' – her father – appears. She gives him a round scolding, perhaps as a wife would her husband, and sends him to bed in his drunken state.

bespoke i.e. Jenny knows that Bradley only has eyes for Lizzie.
A Grenadier A soldier who threw grenades; now used as the title of the first regiment of foot-guards.
Sir Eugene Bountiful Eugene, as always, is self-mocking.
noddle Head.
ain't catching i.e. you won't take infection from it.
object dearest affections i.e. 'The object of the dearest affections of this broken-hearted invalid.' Dickens tries to get the drunken slur of Dolls's speech by these abbreviations.
you prodigal old son Since Jenny treats him as a child, the reference is perhaps appropriate. (See Luke, 15,11–32).
skewers Pins of wood or iron for holding meat compactly together while it is being cooked.
of the world, worldly i.e. she was forced to live with the sordid reality of life as distinct from her dreams.

Chapter 3 A Piece of Work

Veneering is invited to stand for Parliament – that is, if he can put up the money! Twemlow, normally pliable on these occasions, refuses to allow Lord Snigsworth's name to be used as a backer for Veneering, but promises to help him at his club. Veneering goes to see Podsnap, while Mrs Veneering considers it her duty to enlist Lady Tippins's support. Dickens's tone throughout these accounts of frenetic behaviour is highly satirical. Veneering goes down to Pocket-Breaches, speaks, is elected, and is triumphant. Naturally, he uses all the political clichés.

Brittania ... the copper coinage The figure symbolizing Great Britain. She appeared – seated, with a shield and anchor – on the back of old pennies.
Commons i.e. The House of Commons.
put down i.e. in cash, provide.
a Hansom cab Two-wheeled cab, taking two people inside, with the driver mounted behind.
Ophelia and any self-immolating female The heroine of *Hamlet*, who drowns herself; and any self-sacrificing woman.
Life-guards at Waterloo They took a prominent part in the battle fought by the English and Prussians under Wellington and Blücher, against the French under Napoleon (1815).
King Priam i.e. at the storming and firing of Troy (Priam being King of Troy) by the Greeks under Agamemnon.
give me his name i.e. allow me to quote him as a supporter of mine.
gout in the temper i.e. is touchy.
glutinous Sticky.
Pocket-Breaches The name is deliberately ironic, for pocket-boroughs were in the control of one person or family, hence entry to Parliament as a member for a pocket-borough inevitably involved bribery.
proviso i.e. an assurance given.
a hand-gallop i.e. an easy, galloping pace.
Belgravian Borders i.e. on the very edge of fashionable and wealthy society.
we'll bring him in i.e. get him elected.
Tales of the Genii ... Arabian Nights As we can see, Dickens's favourite point of reference when he wants to emphasize the unreality of society – a kind of horror fairy-tale.
plumpers Voters, those who 'plump for' a candidate.

thingummies . . . whatdoyoucallums The vagueness of the terms underlines the lack of any kind of political commitment or policy.
get a man over i.e. to your own side.
jockey a railway i.e. cheat, dupe, swindle.
a Trojan i.e. very hard-working (reference to the defenders of Troy against the Greeks).
capped i.e. bettered.
binns i.e. containing wine.
rarullarulling i.e. rallying.
the lobby In the House of Commons, the large hall wherein members of the public may meet their MPs.
feeble little town hall on crutches i.e. decayed, dilapidated. (But note the echo of Jenny Wren and Silas Wegg.)
He's up i.e. on his feet, about to speak.
the Vessel of State Dickens ransacks the political clichés for Veneering to utter.
underwrite i.e. undertake to finance.

Chapter 4 Cupid Promoted

The Lammles plot to manipulate Georgiana into marriage with Fledgeby. Georgiana visits Sophronia for lunch in her boudoir, Alfred arrives, and Georgiana becomes very nervous and agitated when told of Fledgeby's being 'stricken all of a heap' with admiration for her. The Lammles entertain the prospective young lovers to dinner and have to work hard to sustain the arch conversation and the innuendo which is calculated to involve Fledgeby and Georgiana. The effect is comic and theatrical. Afterwards all four go to the opera.

osteologists Bone specialists.
Pandean pipes Those of Pan, the deity of the woods and pastures, but significantly here – since the comparison is with Podsnap – half goat, half man.
See the conquering Podsnap comes A straight parody of 'See the conquering hero comes'.

boudoir Lady's private room, usually adjoining the bedroom.
she kissed his watch-chain Significant – she has no wish to touch him.
like a pair of compasses The image underlines the mechanical nature of the process.
stricken all of a heap i.e. completely overcome.
too much given to horseflesh i.e. gambling on horse-racing.
the Bourse The foreign money market or stock exchange, especially that of Paris.
indefinably loose i.e. free-living, immoral.
repartee i.e. smart, witty reply.
in such feather . . . next sally i.e. being in such good form . . . his following wit.
like a harlequin Mute character in English and Continental pantomime, usually wearing parti-coloured tights.
the prompt-book Dickens here is deliberately using theatrical terms to underline the theatricality of the situation – the prompt-book is the copy of the play used by the 'prompter' from the side of the stage when actors forget their lines.
usual flow of spirits i.e. customary happy, animated frame of mind.
Very happy i.e. very well expressed.
declare for blue i.e. abandon your loyalty.
craven Cowardly.
circumambient i.e. surrounding.
her cage door Appropriate image, since Georgiana is imprisoned in Podsnappery anyway.
a slow Retriever i.e. an incompetent gundog.
savagely following his little flock Note how inappropriate any rural imagery is to Alfred Lammle, but it heightens the sense of the ridiculous.
apropos Concerning.
and pouring its blood down his throat Strong physical image to stress the unscrupulous nature of Alfred Lammle.
Booby A silly, dull-witted fool.

Chapter 5 Mercury Prompting

Fascination Fledgeby, described as the 'meanest cur existing', is visited by Alfred Lammle for breakfast. Initially Fledgeby proves himself equal to dealing with Lammle but they quarrel, and Lammle the bully, affecting to be very angry, threatens to pull Fledgeby's nose. They then shake hands – Fledgeby humiliated, Lammle genial. Afterwards Fledgeby goes to see Riah, the old-clothes dealer, who takes him up to the garden on his roof. There he sees Jenny Wren and Lizzie Hexam, listening and talking and buying waste from which dolls' clothes can be made. The garden has a kind of symbolic escape from life for Jenny, with her repeated phrase, 'Come up and be dead.'

eulogium Praise.
Registrar-General The authority for recording births and deaths.
Doomsday i.e. the day of Judgement.
had his tools at the grindstone i.e. watched events very carefully.
You're deep and you're ready i.e. you are cunning and prepared for action.
a long-headed fellow i.e. shrewd, possessed, having foresight.
Westminster Hall The seat of justice.
as if I was your doll and puppet Note the range of the irony: the Lammles are doing their best to ensure that Georgiana is just that.
crow i.e. boast, exult.
long odds i.e. outside chances.
L.S.D. Pounds, shillings and pence; British currency superseded by new pounds and pence in 1971.
merry greenwood of Jobbery Forest The associations are with Robin Hood, but as we know Fledgeby we find the language ironic.
pitching-in order i.e. violent.
note of hand i.e. guarantee of payment.

Incessant machinations i.e. unremitting schemes.
scout Reject scorn (an idea).
Jehovah's name The name of God in the Old Testament.
I am game i.e. I am prepared, keen.
folding tablets i.e. sheets of paper.
I have made a little garden there There is an important symbol in the novel, representing as it does the escape into nature from the world's evils, largely caused by money.
in some pilgrimage ... to a prophet's tomb He might be compared with Mordecai in *Daniel Deronda*; both Dickens and George Eliot idealize their Jewish characters, Dickens in part to counterbalance the character of the evil Jew Fagin in *Oliver Twist*.
buy of our damage and waste Note the parallel with the Mounds and the Boffin part of the plot.
you feel as if you were dead i.e. in heaven, in a new life away from the sordid present.
Come back and be dead The phrase carries a terrible irony in the context of the novel, for Fledgeby is 'dead' to the best things in life.
to put any chap up to the fastenings i.e. to tell anyone how to break in.
your weather eye i.e. be alert.

Chapter 6 A Riddle Without an Answer

Eugene Wrayburn and Mortimer Lightwood in the Temple, Mortimer is obviously concerned about Eugene, but the latter says he cannot account for his boredom or his state of mind. Bradley Headstone and Charley arrive; the boy attacks Eugene for instructing his sister (he and Bradley had some plan of their own for her), but Eugene treats them both with contempt. When the boy leaves them together Bradley unleashes a ranting attack on Eugene, who reminds him that the door is open and that he may leave. Mortimer questions him about his feelings for Lizzie – again Eugene is unable to give him an answer.

the Temple, accustomed to tone down both the still life and the human life i.e. the effect of the law, which brings all things dead and living within its orbit.
vagaries i.e. caprices, freaks, whimsical notions.
chum Friend.
Secrétaire ... pigeon-holes Writing desk ... compartments for letters and documents.
little flour-barrel ... coffee-mill i.e. biscuits and coffee.
a tie and a drag upon you i.e. something which had to be done but which you did not want to do.
embodied conundrum i.e. a living, walking riddle, enigma.
monomaniac Insane, obsessed by one subject only.
set-off i.e. counterbalance.
a catechizing infection i.e. a desire to question and find out.

Chapter 7 In Which a Friendly Move is Originated

Silas Wegg is discontented with his life at the Bower, and resents Mr Boffin's frequent evening trips for a reading. Silas invites Mr Venus to visit him at the Bower, and one Saturday evening Mr Venus arrives. Over a glass or so of rum and a pipe they talk. Silas Wegg complains that he feels confined, and that Rokesmith has been set up above him. He and Venus come to an agreement: they will search the Mounds and take anything worth having and share the profits. Should 'papers' come to light, Silas suggests a little blackmail. Naturally, they do not trust each other. Rokesmith arrives with a message from Mr Boffin, to the effect that he had not intended Silas Wegg to be tied by his unexpected visits and will, in future, take a chance on finding him in. Silas and Venus are somewhat the worse for wear after a number of 'mixings'.

old Jamaikey warm i.e. rum.
ha'porthetically ... penn'orthetically Wegg means 'hypothetically'; but Venus takes the pronunciation seriously, and punningly extends the ha'penny to penny.

Mix for yourself i.e. your drink.
perform upon a pipe i.e. smoke.
Charity . . . cardinal virtue by the skirts Note how the personification has the effect of making Wegg all the more unscrupulous.
talking-over stranger i.e. one who thinks himself superior.
Jacks-in-boxes i.e. which spring out suddenly.
in lights i.e. in certain ways.
apostrophe Exclamatory phrase or address.
chiromancy Palmistry.
British Oak Extending the nautical associations of the song – compare the phrase 'hearts of oak', meaning 'steadfast, brave'.
codicils Supplementary additions changing wills.
See into what wonderful maudlin refuges The omniscient author commenting on Wegg's capacity to mislead himself.
the minion of fortune One of Wegg's favourite phrases to indicate the fickle nature of time and fortune; hence ironic.

Chapter 8 In Which an Innocent Elopement Occurs

Bella is now at the Boffins, helping to put Mrs Boffin right socially. Bella discusses with Mr Boffin the curiously unsociable habits of John Rokesmith; John talks to Bella, and offers to deliver messages to her parents, but Bella informs him that she has decided to go home the next day. Nevertheless, Rokesmith makes her uneasy. She goes home, but meets some hostility for her neglect on the part of her eccentric mother. There follows an extraordinary, distorted and quite unpleasant family row, the histrionics of Mrs Wilfer being particularly impressive. Rokesmith delivers to Bella a purse containing fifty pounds, which she determines to spend on her father. She takes him out to Greenwich for the day, treats him, gives him great affection, but confirms her intention to marry money.

Legacy Duty Tax imposed on the beneficiary of a will.
Be it this history's part Once again, note the omniscient intervention in the narrative.

when we came home . . . to hand us out Note, too, the move into the intimate and graphic present which conveys Rokesmith's concern.

stipendiary girl i.e. paid servant.

her heraldic manner i.e. full of self-importance as of hereditary right.

a female Lieutenant of the Tower i.e. of London, where state prisoners were kept. But note the bubbling humour of the idea!

a slap-up gal in a bang-up chariot i.e. a pretty girl in a fine carriage.

Saveloy . . . Small Germans A seasoned dried sausage; small sausages.

elegant turn-out i.e. fashionable carriage.

Dead March in Saul A funeral march written by Handel.

hornpipe Sailors' dance (Trad).

black diamonds i.e. coal.

bark A sailing ship.

Cleopatra (69–30 BC) The legendary Egyptian queen who captivated Mark Antony.

red coats and blue jackets i.e. soldiers and sailors.

Cashmere shawls From the fine soft wool of the belly of the Kashmir goat native to Northern India.

the Sultan's tub of water Probably a reference to the story in the *Arabian Nights' Tales*: when the thirsty put their heads into the tub to drink, the water dried up. In other words, Pa Wilfer is perfectly happy to be carried along by Bella's wonderful stories – which he knows, of course, would 'dry up' in reality.

Chapter 9 In which the Orphan Makes his Will

Sloppy arrives at the Boffins' house, bringing news of little Johnny's decline. Mrs Higden has kept silent about it, and Mrs Boffin is upset by this. They set off for Mrs Higden's, buying, en route, toys for Johnny, including a remarkable toy horse, which he examines. He also looks at the 'boofer lady' (Bella). Betty does not want him to be taken from her and is distressed and angry at the idea; then she quietly relents, and Johnny and his toys are taken to the Childrens' Hospital. Rokesmith realizes that the little boy is going to die and determines to return to his bedside that night. The toys, including Johnny's, are all left out while the children sleep, and Johnny's last act is to have his animals placed for the little boy in the next bed. He kisses Rokesmith, telling him that the kiss is for the 'boofer lady'. He dies, and the scene is as moving as the death of little Paul in *Dombey and Son*.

must have took 'em from i.e. must have caught them from.
partickler Particularly.
wot you couldn't kiver i.e. couldn't cover.
their striking in'ards that's to be kep' off i.e. they are serious when they affect the inside.
rayther a tight time i.e. had been overworked.
unbeknownst i.e. without anyone knowing.
God save the Queen and Con-found their politics Here Dickens is taking a line from the National Anthem in order to express his fervent loyalty to the suffering poor.
rumble Back part of carriage arranged as a seat.
the Power and the Glory Betty's way of referring to the Lord's Prayer ('For Thine is the Kingdom, the Power and the Glory').
kill the Pretty i.e. the child.
'crops up' i.e. occurs.
overcharged breast i.e. his feelings of grief.
Children's Hospital The Great Ormond Street Hospital for Sick Children.
Moorish tumblers i.e. acrobats.

Chapter 10 A Successor

The burial of Johnny, and the transparent delight of Silas Wegg, who considers himself the real orphan. Rokesmith and Mrs Boffin talk sympathetically, and Mrs Boffin wants the name 'John Harmon' dropped since they had bestowed it on little Johnny. Then Sloppy arrives and is presented to them in his new suit. Mrs Boffin offers to take care of him for life; he is grateful, but also mindful of the fact that he will have to continue to do Mrs Higden's 'turning'.

say out of nine and thirty Probably a sly reference to the thirty-nine articles, first drawn up in 1562, to which clergymen of the Church of England must subscribe.
pirouette i.e. spinning round on one foot or the point of the toe.
kept-down i.e. held in check.
Ancoar i.e. encore – do it again.
a perfect Argus The fabulous creature of Greek mythology who had one hundred eyes.
dooty . . . faviours Duty . . . favours.
Striking right out, mum i.e. getting stronger and improving all the time.
turned for i.e. he must do the mangling.

Chapter 11 Some Affairs of the Heart

Here we are taken back to Miss Peecher, with the schoolmistress indulging herself in dreams about the schoolmaster and interrogating Mary Anne about him. Then Bradley appears, makes off to see Lizzie, and leaves the key with Miss Peecher. Arrived at the doll's dressmaker's, he finds Jenny Wren there by herself. Then, when Lizzie arrives, he examines her about the teaching she is having, and she reveals to him that she is being instructed by a competent teacher. She obviously resents his interference, though in part he claims to be speaking for Charley. The physical revulsion she feels for Headstone is again evident. Afterwards Jenny, by encouraging Lizzie, draws from her a confession of her love for Eugene Wrayburn.

had never been examined or certificated out of her Another sardonic comment by Dickens on the educational system of the day.

and the nightingales tuned up Note the humorous tone – almost like the romantic background music in a film.

Vesuvius and Aetna Famous volcanoes.

Ganges and Nile The great rivers of India and Egypt respectively.

in certain smouldering natures This sufficiently defines Bradley's passionate responses, but he also gives the impression of suffering from epilepsy or a similar condition.

lighted lucifer-matches Matches were called 'lucifers' at the time; the oblique reference is to Bradley Headstone's passionate nature.

'The hollow down by the flare?' A reminder of Lizzie's past gazing into the fire, in which she saw Charley's future.

O my blessed children Jenny's dream is full of the innocence and love that Lizzie needs to sustain her in the difficult times ahead.

Chapter 12 More Birds of Prey

Another return, this time to Rogue Riderhood. Pleasant Riderhood, his daughter (who is a pawnbroker, among other things) is described. She is a much better person than Rogue, though certainly with an eye always on the main chance. One evening a man calls upon her and asks for her father. He reveals that he has been there before; and a mysterious conversation follows in which he shows that he is familiar with Riderhood's trade, and has himself been drugged and robbed on one occasion. Rogue returns, drinks with the stranger, who exerts an ominous power over him. The stranger draws the talk round to Hexam and his surviving children. He says that he will get Rogue to sign a paper to the effect that Hexam is blameless in regard to the Harmon murder.

a Leaving Shop i.e. goods would be left there, and if not reclaimed after a certain time, they would become the property of the owner of the shop.

as a blind i.e. an activity that diverts attention from what is really going on.
principal and interest i.e. the original sum plus the interest payable by the depositor.
oakum-coloured Oakum is the loose fibre obtained from picking old rope – probably grey-coloured is implied here.
with Jack i.e. with sailors.
the parties i.e. those involved.
Poll Parrot i.e. talkative.
Fortunatus' goblet Fortunatus got anything he wished for, but was cursed in the end.
On Leaving i.e. things at the shop.
Old Bailey The Central Criminal Court.
pint Point.
trumped-up False.
perwerse jade Obstinate slut.
hocussed Drugged.
foreswore Perjured.

Chapter 13 A Solo and a Duett

The visitor leaves Limehouse Hole, and is revealed to be Julius Handford alias John Rokesmith. He ponders about his life-in-death by Limehouse Churchyard, and then tells his own story in the form of a monologue (the 'Solo' of the Chapter-heading). His resemblance to the seaman George Radfoot is explained: they had arranged to come ashore together and to seek out Bella (without Harmon-Handford-Rokesmith revealing who he is); then Harmon is duped by Radfoot and Riderhood. Drugged, he half realizes that Radfoot has been mistaken for him and robbed. Harmon and Radfoot are flung into the water and Harmon survives. He recovers in the public house for some forty-eight hours; twelve days later he sees the corpse of Radfoot at the police station. He ponders on the possibility of bringing John Harmon back to life; he loves Bella (despite her nature) and also thinks well of the Boffins, and decides to leave well (or ill) alone. He continues in his role of John Rokesmith; when he gets back he finds that Bella wishes to talk to him. She tells him that he must not pay formal attentions to her; after this he determines not to reveal that he is John Harmon. Bella is a little put out by her own 'wilful' behaviour.

kennels Gutters.
doubles i.e. going back on our tracks.
Sultan Muslim sovereign.
Home Goddess i.e. perfection of domestic happiness.
Alpine range The most extensive mountain system in Europe.
Sexton Rokesmith Often the sexton of a church is the grave-digger; hence the association in Rokesmith's – and the author's – mind.

Chapter 14 Strong of Purpose

Rokesmith is still pondering on his dilemma, and the next day he meets R. Wilfer. The latter tells him that Bella will marry for money, and this deepens his brooding. Betty Higden arrives at the Boffin mansion to tell Rokesmith that Sloppy cannot do two jobs. She proposes to run away from Sloppy, so that he can benefit from the Boffins' treatment of him. She is provided with material to sell on her journey; and Rokesmith further determines to get a confession from Rogue Riderhood. He cleverly decides to take Sloppy to Bradley Headstone in order to open that particular channel to Hexam. Bradley agrees to undertake the teaching of Sloppy, but becomes somewhat overwrought when Lizzie is mentioned. Afterwards Betty is provided by Rokesmith with a letter giving the Boffins' address to contact should she fall sick. She also carries with her 'the man in the Guards', a memento of Johnny, 'away from paralysis and pauperism'.

black kings are cheap i.e. commonplace.
a Manchester pair of braces i.e. made in Manchester.

I got the start of him i.e. I was up before he was.
afeerd Frightened.
brick up in the Unions i.e. imprison in the workhouses.
fit out a basket i.e. in which to carry her knitting, which she will sell.
contradiction i.e. go against my own nature.
want to be of a piece like i.e. act consistently.
stanch Steadfast.
the books of Charities i.e. set up by public people or 'do-gooders', and of course always asking for money.
warm i.e. angry.
They ain't Pills, or Hair-Washes ... to be puffed in that way Mr Boffin is launching an attack on Charities that advertise (puff) themselves like the goods he describes above.
right as a trivet Steady, in good health or situation.

Chapter 15 The Whole Case so Far

Bradley and Charley set off, going to Leadenhall Street in order to 'lurk' for Lizzie. When they meet her they go to a churchyard; Charley intends to leave Bradley and Lizzie together, and does so. Bradly confesses to Lizzie that she is the 'ruin' of him and becomes more and more impassioned in the expression of his feelings. He proposes to her, if such it can be called; she rejects him and, as he damages his knuckles against the stone, he prays that he may never kill 'him' – obviously meaning Eugene Wrayburn. When Bradley has gone, Charley upbraids Lizzie, but says that she will not disgrace him, since he will have nothing more to do with her. After he has left, Riah sees Lizzie and hastens to assist her. On the way they meet Eugene Wrayburn who accompanies them – not without flippant commentary – home.

chit Saucy young girl.
flinging his heart's blood down before her Note that Dickens seeks to convey Bradley's passion by extreme physical references from now on.

breaking up the waters ... our pictures in the fire Notice how these two images, almost together, reflect Lizzie's life as rowing assistant to her father, and warm unselfish helpmeet to her brother.

Mysteries of Udolpho The novel of that name by Ann Radcliffe; in the Gothic tradition, and published in 1794.

Mr Aaron ... the Synagogue The name 'Aaron' was often applied to a Jew, and the Synagogue is the Jewish place of worship. Eugene is being unkind and unfeeling.

Chapter 16 An Anniversary Occasion

Now to Twemlow in St James's Yard, getting ready to dine out and to meet 'Fledgeby', the occasion being the Lammles' anniversary breakfast to 'celebrate' their marriage. There is a splendid irony about the whole chapter, seen particularly in the treatment of Lady Tippins. The machinations about Georgiana continue; and conversation veers again towards the Harmon murder. Mortimer Lightwood now picks up the story, underlining the vindication of Gaffer Hexam and the disappearance of his daughter Lizzie. The satirical presentation of Veneering's speechifying continues, but after Lammle's own speech Mrs Lammle asks for a private word with Twemlow. Though she is being watched, Sophronia begs Twemlow to save Georgiana from his undesirable relation Fledgeby. This is a remarkable and dramatic confession of her own way of life, and Twemlow goes home bewildered.

toilette Process of getting ready.

the Graces The three beautiful goddesses of Greek mythology responsible for bestowing beauty and charm.

diurnal Daily.

the new crust hardens i.e. her make-up, all the preparations, are ready.

sumptuousity i.e. extravagance.

ukase Edict of Tzarist Russian government, any arbitrary order.

Guy Earl of Warwick ... dun cow ... Flitch of Bacon An odd mixture of sound rather than sense. Guy of Warwick, the legendary Saxon hero, overcame the famous dun cow on a heath near Warwick; but the Dunmow Flitch of bacon – the ceremony still exists – was awarded to the couple who could best prove that they were still happily married. (This dates from the mid fifteenth century.)

turn out i.e. displace.

mastication and deglutition Chewing and swallowing – superior words for a superior lady.

that being the tone of the House of Commons Another ironic aside at the debilitating effect of politics.

I'll tell a story/Of Jack a Manory A story that ended almost as soon as it began. It was much used by children's nurses.

Bear ... Beauty ... Beast Again an association with fairy tales is being set up – and one supposes that Lady Tippins is herself something of a fairy tale.

gradually toning into the Parliamentary sing-song Again the ironic tone is evident.

gammon and spinach i.e. nonsense.

oratorical Pegasus Pegasus was the winged horse of Greek mythology – hence the association here with the 'high-flown' language of Veneering.

Genie of the cheek ... rubbing The reference is to Aladdin and his rubbing of the wonderful lamp, which caused the Genie to appear and carry out his wishes.

puffed-up i.e. conceited.

the Golden Age The first of four ages when, it is believed, men were happy and innocent.

flitch of bacon See note on the Dunmow Flitch above – all ironic in view of the Lammles' unhappy marriage.

flushed letter-cart i.e. red, the colour of the mail cart.

Book 3 A Long Lane

Chapter 1 Lodgers in Queer Street

Armed with the accounts, Riah walks to Albany on a raw foggy morning. He waits patiently for Fledgeby to answer his knock; after a while he is admitted. Fledgeby promptly returns to bed. Again Riah waits patiently, but this time in front of a fire. Fledgeby finally rises and pours coffee for himself but not for the old man. He then orders Riah to prove the balance in hand, which is correct. Alfred Lammle arrives with a note he has received from Podsnap, stating that from now on all communication between their two families shall cease. Fledgeby later urges Lammle not to fall into the hands of Pubsey & Co, in the form of Riah. Lammle leaves and Fledgeby vows that he will bring him down. He discovers that Riah is hiding Lizzie, and learns of Eugene Wrayburn's involvement. He then sends Riah on his way and goes out into the fog.

to get their heads above the foggy sea Note this unifying atmospheric image – part of the water imagery present in all sections of the plot. (Compare the fog at the opening of *Bleak House*.)
enfolding a gigantic catarrh A personification that conveys the difficulty of breathing in a city fog.
Turkish slippers ... Turkish trousers i.e. those that turn up ... those that billow out but fit tightly round the ankle.
sweating a pound i.e. shaking up the coins in a bag. this causes some of the metal to 'sweat'; later, when the bag is sold, its metal residue ensures a good price.
cut things so fine i.e. take such a risk.
Jerusalem palaver i.e. Jewish talk.
Queer Street is full of lodgers i.e. what a number of people in debt there are!
Pump of Israel A derogatory, anti-semitic term.
we'll mark that person i.e. we'll take note of him.

promissory note A document that indicates a promise to pay.
flayers and grinders i.e. they will punish you and insist that you pay up.
Don't break out i.e. don't get angry.
she don't lay it upon me i.e. she doesn't blame me.
I'll bowl you down i.e. I'll make you suffer, make you pay.
regular pity the sorrows The opening lines of a poem by Thomas Moss called *The Beggar's Petition.*
Patriarchs Fathers and rulers of families and tribes in Israel.
your spoon in the soup i.e. your interest in this affair.
Honour Among Jews Fledgeby's satirical version of 'honour among thieves'.
the circle was fast darkening Things were getting worse for her.
circular i.e. devious, cunning.
Judah A reference to one of the tribes of Israel, a synonym for 'Jew'.
A tidy shot ... a Jew brought down with it A clean hit ... and I have got the Jew where I want him.
put him in the light ... brought him down plump Got him against the light ... got him suddenly.
ablutions ... anointing himself Note the effect of the language.
quacks i.e. fakes, whom Fledgeby accepts as well as moneylenders.

Chapter 2 A Respected Friend in a New Aspect

Riah collects Jenny Wren and they set off on a walk. On the way she confesses how much she misses Lizzie; she also indulges in a marvellous fantasy about her dolls, having seen a number of them displayed in a shop window. They arrive eventually at the Six Jolly Fellowship Porters and see Miss Abbey Potterson. They speak of Lizzie, and show Miss Abbey that Hexam is cleared of any involvement in the murder of 'John Harmon'. Miss Abbey asks Riah and Jenny to tell Lizzie that she can always stay with her (Abbey). Meanwhile, there is an accident in the fog, a steamer having run down a wherry. The apparently lifeless form of Rogue Riderhood is brought into the room, with Riah and Jenny Wren looking on.

blanks i.e. lottery tickets that gain no prizes.
it would start up a coach and six A continuation of the Cinderella associations.
copper-coloured men in red ... fiery furnace Dolls's alcoholism underlined in this vision.
mooney i.e. absent-minded, slow to understand.
baste Sew loosely together with large tacking stitches. (The Americans still say 'baste' for 'tack'.)
avocation i.e. employment.
Cape of Good Hope At the southernmost tip of South Africa.
shrub Often rumshrub, since it was made with lemon, sugar, water and rum.
drags Apparatus for dredging, recovering.
She was the Murderer Some indication, conveyed through this personification, of what is shouted at the steamer.

Chapter 3 The Same Respected Friend in More Aspects than One

A doctor and Riderhood's daughter are quickly sent for by Miss Abbey; there is thought to be little hope for Riderhood. Pleasant arrives and Riderhood, having been brought round by the doctor, stirs. Those round him go down to have a drink, but Pleasant remains. Eventually, restored to his normal bad humour, Riderhood goes off after his 'turn-up with Death.'

it is the outer husk Notice that Dickens has deliberately gone into the present tense to make the narrative more graphic.
His gills looks rum i.e. the flesh below his jaws and ears looks unhealthy – he is having difficulty in breathing.

the Fates In Greek mythology the three goddesses who presided over the destiny of individuals.
bust her i.e. curse her (the steamer).
a rare lot i.e. a distinguished group (heavy sarcasm).
ring ... turn-up The comparison is with boxing – a fight with death.

Chapter 4 A Happy Return of the Day

This is the twenty-fifth wedding anniversary of the Wilfers, with Bella returning for the day. She spies on Rokesmith's room (the guest has placed it at their disposal) and, among other things, finds the placard of the murdered man. Bella takes over the cooking, George Sampson (not courting Lavvy) arrives, and Mrs Wilfer, as is her wont, indulges in dark reminiscences throughout the meal. The principal focus of her misery is her marriage to R. Wilfer. Afterwards the latter walks with Bella, who tells him that Rokesmith has proposed to her and that Mortimer Lightwood would do so if given the chance. She also says that the Boffins will see her well provided for when she marries, but reveals that Mr Boffin is changing for the worse under the influence of 'money, money, money'.

put one another out of countenance i.e. got on each other's nerves.
portfolio Case for keeping loose sheets of paper.
decamped i.e. left.
entrenchments ... flag of truce Note the ironic continuation of military images to define domestic conflict.
King Frederick of Prussia (1740–86) Here a reference to the famous Potsdam regiment, most of the men being over seven feet in height.
a knock-knee'd mind i.e. muddled, not clear.
money, money, money ... can make of life The theme of the novel sardonically underlined.

Chapter 5 The Golden Dustman Falls into Bad Company

When Bella gets back to the Boffins, Rokesmith's salary is being fixed. He is to have £200 per annum, but all his time is to be placed at Mr Boffin's service. He talks of how Rokesmith must keep his place, and Bella notices the greed on Mr Boffin's face. He urges Bella to live only to make money – 'There's a golden ball at your feet.' After this, he begins to collect books on the lives of 'any old characters who may have been misers'. Meanwhile Mrs Lammle affects to be fascinated by Bella, though the latter dislikes Lammle and mistrusts his wife. Unfortunately, she confides to Mrs Lammle the fact that Rokesmith has proposed to her. Later Bella witnesses further evidence of Boffin's meanness; for it is established that Rokesmith is to move into the Boffin household as a means of saving money, and thus his time can certainly be Mr Boffin's.

passing through the furnace . . . coming out dross i.e. was Boffin passing through his testing time and demonstrating that he was small-minded, and weak?

specification i.e. discussion of terms of reference.

You'll make money of your good looks Advice that right-thinking Bella comes to reject.

There's a golden ball at your feet i.e. life is full of opportunities for you. There is much play on the word 'golden' in the novel, some of it merely descriptive (the 'golden shower' of Jenny's hair, for instance); and some ironic, as here and in the 'golden' dustman.

Annual Register A survey of foreign and domestic news, with reference to important people.

Don Quixote The Hero of the great novel of that name whose head was turned by tales of knight-errantry. It was written by Miguel de Cervantes (1547–1616).

a Judas order i.e. false and treacherous, after Judas Iscariot.

Mr Elwes . . . Daniel Dancer Celebrated misers who appear in

The Wonderful and Scientific Museum (1803–20), a copy of which Dickens possessed.

Chapter 6 The Golden Dustman Falls into Worse Company

We learn about the feelings of Silas Wegg at being, as he thinks, supplanted by Rokesmith, and also his resentment of the new literary undertakings he has to serve up for Mr Boffin. Mr Wegg talks to Venus, who is thoroughly disgruntled by the lack of action. Then Boffin arrives with a number of books, including those about the lives of the misers, and Wegg's evening task, in front of Venus, is to read about these models for Mr Boffin. There are deliberate associations with the Mounds, while one contains a reference to a will. Next Mr Boffin produces a lantern and goes around the Mounds, spied upon as he does so by Wegg and Venus. They watch Boffin unearth a bottle; then he reveals to Wegg that he is selling the Mounds next day; Venus has to restrain Wegg from going after him.

in great dudgeon High offence.

Rollins Ancient History Dickens had a copy of this, which first appeared in English in 1740. Its subject was the ancient Egyptians.

Alexander the Macedonian i.e. 'the Great', born at Pella in 356 BC.

The Wars of the Jews Strictly, *The Jewish War* by Flavius Josephus.

Plutarch ... Lives The celebrated Greek biographer, whose lives of famous Greeks and Romans established his fame (AD 50–120).

And you needn't Mr Venus Again, Wegg's rendering of the fifth verse of 'Auld Lang Syne', by Robert Burns (1759–96).

Rome ... wasn't built in a day Originally from the French (about 1190) meaning that nothing can be achieved all at once.

Charge, Chester, charge From the poem, *Marmion* (1808) by Sir Walter Scott (1771–1832), written before he began the Waverley novels in 1814.

Caulfield's ... Wilson's See previous chapter. These were published in 1821.

Dancer ... Taylor ... Wood i.e. misers.

like the four-and-twenty fiddlers Perhaps Mr Boffin is thinking of the four-and-twenty blackbirds of the nursery rhyme.

Merryweather's Lives and Anecdotes of Misers Published in 1850. Dickens had a copy in his own library.

snuffers i.e. for trimming a candle.

regimen Diet.

escretoires (A misspelling of 'escritoires', from the French.) Strictly, writing-desks, but obviously here a hiding-place is referred to.

petrefaction Paralysis, stupefaction.

crown-piece A coin worth five shillings (25 pence).

serpentining walk i.e. twisting and turning.

holler i.e. hollow.

the Dutchman is said to keep his Courage in A reference to the expression 'Dutch courage', still used today to allude to strong drink (which, the drinker hopes, will give him courage).

It has fetched a penny i.e. I've sold it for quite a sum.

rummaged i.e. sorted through for valuables.

Chapter 7 The Friendly Move Takes Up a Strong Position

Wegg tells Venus that he has previously found a cash-box with papers in it – John Harmon's will – apparently leaving one small Mound to Boffin, the rest to the Crown. Wegg further asserts that he has checked that this was the last will, and advises going to Venus's place so that they can both inspect it. They do, and Venus insists on having his share of the will and adopts, despite his language, a threatening attitude towards Wegg. They discuss the next step, which is blackmail on the strength of the will, with the addition of a careful eye to be kept on the Mounds, particularly at night, when they can search what has been left over during the day. Wegg executes a masterly parody of 'Home Sweet Home', Venus reveals that the object of his love is Pleasant Riderhood, and Wegg leaves, brooding on the fact that he has taken Venus into partnership. Next Silas, having cursed the Golden Dustman, watches the little Mound being carted away.

Usurper i.e. someone who is taking over.
what a speaking countenance is yours i.e. your face conveys what you are thinking.
sap – pur – IZE i.e. a surprise.
All's Well Another popular song (by Thomas Dibdin, 1771–1841), with Wegg's own alterations.
to beguile the monotony of a literary life A masterly affectation on the part of Wegg.
were yet in abeyance i.e. not yet made.
the trophies of my art Venus is certainly surrounded by a weird collection of complete and incomplete bodies.
compo-one i.e. compound one. The bones of more than one person are involved.
bile i.e. boil.
the sharp sword i.e. the threat.
flagrant article Wegg is carried away; he means 'fragrant'.
Home Sweet Home From the opera *Clari* (1823), by John Howard Payne (1791–1882) and Sir Henry R. Bishop (1786–1855). It has since become one of the most popular sentimental songs.
a nice pair of rattlesnakes Rather an ominous choice, in view of the conversation.
spoliation i.e. plunder, pillage.

Chapter 8 The End of a Long Journey

This opens with an indictment of the suffering of the poor; then moves on to the specific example of Betty Higden. Betty fears charity more than anything else; on one occasion during her journey she faints, being picked up by bystanders. On another occasion she thinks that she sees the forms of her dead children on a barge. The lock-keeper (Riderhood) lets Betty go on, but takes her remaining money as the price for not reporting her to the Parish. Her terrible journey continues – 'like a criminal afraid of being taken' – and she finally lies down at the foot of a tree that reminds her of the foot of the Cross. She is found by Lizzie Hexam, who reads the letter and, of course, recognizes the names. Betty dies in this most moving scene.

My lords and gentlemen and honourable boards This invocation, a part of Dickens's stylistic method throughout, links government, society and dust; and indicts the whole fabric of mismanagement that can forsake the Betty Higdens of its world.
the young river, dimpled like a young child Symbolizing Betty's care of children throughout her long, precarious existence.
the Relieving Officer One appointed to administer the Poor Law relief payments.
the Good Samaritan See Luke, 10,33 onwards.
afeard i.e. frightened.
comforter Long scarf.
dropping diamonds i.e. of water.
truckle-bed Low bed on wheels.
Alfred David The use of this version of the word 'affidavit' gives away the speaker's identity.
argueyfied i.e. argued.
like a criminal afraid of being taken A striking comparison.

Chapter 9 Somebody Becomes the Subject of a Prediction

The lonely burial of Betty Higden, with Lizzie saying how kind her Jewish friends have been to her. Bella and Rokesmith watch her closely, both having been asked by the

Boffins to report on Lizzie on their return. Meanwhile, Bella and John Rokesmith get on much better together, and she questions him about Mr Boffin's treatment of him. After that they walk by the 'mirror' of the river. Then Bella calls on Lizzie, talks about Lizzie's secrecy, while Lizzie in her turn wants to know who was responsible for clearing her father in the supposed Harmon murder. Bella asks Lizzie to become her friend, and Lizzie confides in her sufficiently to tell her the story of Bradley Headstone. Again Lizzie virtually confesses her love for Eugene; then the two girls part affectionately. Bella returns to Rokesmith and takes his arm; they get on a train from Oxfordshire, for it was into that county that Betty Higden had wandered.

warn't Was not.
and force myself to act a part Certainly ironic, in view of the 'parts' Rokesmith has had to play.
But the great serene mirror of the river Note the peacefulness of this, and compare it with the other river references in the novel.
Judaical Jewish.
exordium Introduction (usually to a discourse).
willed-away i.e. disposed of by the will.
Tragic Muse Melpomene was the muse or goddess of Tragedy.
living girdle i.e. waist.
green eye . . . red one Expressive way of indicating the signals.

Chapter 10 Scouts Out

Jenny Wren and Eugene Wrayburn are together, with the former's 'child' the worse for drink. Eugene is obviously trying to get Lizzie's address from Jenny, but not succeeding. Later he goes off towards Charing Cross and a little later still sees Jenny's 'bad boy' trying to cross the road. Eugene meets Mortimer Lightwood and discusses Lizzie's disappearance, suggesting that Riah had spirited Lizzie away. Eugene is determined to find her and, in doing so, to discover his own intentions. There is a knock, and 'Mr Dolls' comes in; he is supplied with rum – and fumigated – and begins talking haphazardly. He can, however, trace Lizzie's whereabouts through the letters that have passed between her and Jenny, and is pressed by Eugene to do so. Later Eugene reveals that he is himself being constantly followed and spied upon and he knows that his pursuer is Bradley Headstone. He claims that he has led Bradley a merry dance all over London, and asks Mortimer to join in the fun with him that night. Eugene deliberately arranges for them to encounter Bradley. That night Mortimer is sleepless, haunted by the torment he sees in Bradley's face.

swipey Tipsy.
rating i.e. telling off.
Deration Slurred speech for 'consideration'.
Italian Opera i.e. to look at fashion there (so that she can make dolls' clothes to match it).
Shylock The main character in Shakespeare's *Merchant of Venice*, who insists on redeeming his bond for a pound of flesh but is legally defeated by Portia, disguised as a lawyer.
pastiles i.e. used for fumigation, clearing the air.
Er give up that drection i.e. to tell you where she's gone.
ill-used vidual i.e. badly treated person.
Blown up i.e. told off.
Mint money i.e. a lot of money.
Lerrers i.e. letters.
have it out with him i.e. fight him.
shameful scout i.e. degrading spy.
Don't be like Patience on a mantelpiece frowning at Dolls See *Twelfth Night*, Act 2, Scene 4, where Cesario (Viola) obliquely says that she is herself 'like Patience on a Monument/Smiling at grief'. (Jane Austen uses the same quotation early in *Northanger Abbey*.)
and being gone you are a man again Dickens has had a rush of Shakespeare to the head; this is an echo of *Macbeth*, Act 3,

Scene 4, at the banquet scene where the ghost of Banquo appears to Macbeth.

Observe the dyer's hand You are taking on the colour of your profession.

With Venetian mystery Venice is a labyrinth of canals, eerie and sinister to the stranger.

hope springs eternal in the scholastic breast According to Alexander Pope (1688–1744), 'Hope springs eternal in the human breast.'

hipped Depressed (can also mean 'obsessed').

Yoicks Hunting cry.

rather difficult country about Bethnal Green Eugene is mocking; it is not difficult hunting country but an area in which he can make it difficult for Bradley to follow them.

Got your wind i.e. are you ready for the chase?

Chapter 11 In the Dark

We witness the restlessness of Bradley Headstone on the one hand, and of Miss Peecher on the other. Bradley approaches the watchman at the Temple gate, gets into the chambers occupied by Mortimer and Eugene and stops outside the door. When he comes out he meets another man going in on business with Mr Lightwood. This is none other than Rogue Riderhood, who reveals that he is now a deputy lock-keeper. He is still intent on claiming damages from the steamer that knocked him down. Bradley thus knows who he is and where he comes from, and he gives him five shillings; Riderhood does not understand why. Bradley questions him about Lizzie Hexam; Rogue, before returning to the lock, promises to keep an eye open for Eugene and Lizzie. He now recognizes Headstone's jealousy.

the performance of his ... educational tricks Note the sardonic tone in this appraisal.

Hooroar i.e. Hooray.

I kisses the book i.e. the Bible.
stifficate i.e. certificate.
agin Against.
along of you i.e. about you.
pisons Poisons.
being sweet upon her i.e. in love with her.
passion-wasted nightbird Note that this description is equivalent to the 'bird of prey' associations earlier.
a scholastic huntsman clad for the field A deepening of the irony when we recall Eugene Wrayburn's hunting metaphors.

Chapter 12 Meaning Mischief

Breakfast and acid conversation between the Lammles. They are heavily in debt, though they believe that for the moment the furniture has been saved by the intervention of Fledgeby. Sophronia suggests that they seek financial help from the Boffins, but asserts that they must first get rid of Rokesmith. Her scheme is to disclose to the Boffins that the Secretary has had the effrontery to propose to Bella; and then to get Lammle appointed to the position of Secretary. Alfred suggests that Bella too should be ousted but Sophronia rejects the idea. She also uses her influence to persuade Fledgeby to hold off Riah; but Fledgeby, with calculated and inflexible determination, promptly goes off to see Riah, to make him act.

blown upon i.e. exposed.
burst up i.e. be insolvent.
Wide-Awake Fledgeby's endearing way of being sarcastic at the expense of Riah's non-activity.

Chapter 13 Give a Dog a Bad Name, and Hang Him

Fledgeby is left in the counting house, when Jenny arrives in search of Riah. Fledgeby blackens Riah's name to her and disclaims any connection with Pubsey and Co. The next visitor, surprisingly, is Twemlow, also in search of Riah. Fledgeby damns Riah under the pretence of standing by the Lammles. He is also moved to offer aid to Twemlow (who is Fledgeby's distant relative), when Twemlow reveals that Riah is demanding payment of a debt incurred many years ago when he gave his name as guarantor. Fledgeby holds out small comfort, telling Twemlow that he (Twemlow) may have to go to prison. When Riah does finally arrive, Fledgeby makes sure that he puts into operation his orders with regard to Twemlow. Of course Fledgeby is the villain of the piece, but he makes it appear that it is Riah who is responsible for the enforcement of severity. But Jenny, listening, feels that her 'godmother' is a wolf, and further believes that he may have betrayed Lizzie, hence the title of the chapter.

The old cock in black i.e. the old fellow (Riah).
dodges i.e. tricks.
as a toucher Almost, nearly.
bitingest and tightest i.e. not to be put off and very mean.
Straduarius i.e. Stradivarius, from the famous maker of violins, Antonio Stradivari (1644?–1737).
a Madonna A painting of the Virgin Mary.
Don't play the tune of the trade i.e. don't pretend that you are something you are not.
slap down i.e. at once.
kick-up i.e. disturbance.
You are the Wolf in the Forest We are back to the story of Little Red Ridinghood.

Chapter 14 Mr Wegg prepares a Grindstone for Mr Boffin's Nose

Venus now regularly attends the readings about the misers, and is always seen home by the artful Wegg, who likes inspecting their valuable piece of paper. But Venus arranges secretly to see Mr Boffin on business, and when he does so tells him of the deal he has done with Wegg. Boffin suggests that Venus should pretend to be still part of that deal, but Venus initially refuses, just as he refuses to yield up the will. When Wegg is heard outside, Boffin hides; Wegg enters damning his employer, and telling Venus that Sloppy has been put in to supervise the loading of the Mounds. After a thorough diatribe Wegg leaves; Boffin emerges; and Venus, after much persuasion, agrees to continue saying nothing to Wegg. He also promises to report back to Mr Boffin. The latter, on the way home, is accosted by Mrs Lammle, who is affectedly distressed. Mr Boffin joins her in her carriage.

checked off i.e. sure that everything is correct.
turned under the screw i.e. responded to the pressure.
labouring bark ... perfect archipelago ... soundings Note the running sea imagery in this part of the novel, another unifying effect.
got out of the square i.e. left the straight and narrow course.
jintly i.e. jointly.
And I will pledge with mine From 'Drink to me only' by Ben Jonson (1573–1637).
foxey old grasper and griper i.e. cunning old miser and complainer.
Ecod Euphemism for 'By God'.
jog his terrors i.e. cause him to be fearful.
hydrocephalic i.e. affected by water on the brain (remember that they are in jars).
When the heart of a man From *The Beggar's Opera* by John Gay (1685–1732).

Chapter 15 The Golden Dustman at his Worst

The morning after seeing Mrs Lammle, Boffin displays his displeasure with Rokesmith. In the afternoon he sends for him and, in front of Bella and Mrs Boffin, accuses him of being an adventurer seeking wealth by feigning affection for Bella. Rokesmith asserts his love for Bella during this unpleasant scene, accepts his discharge and the insults, and makes as if to leave. Bella is greatly upset by being 'righted' in this way, and begs to be made poor again. She turns somewhat hysterically on the Golden Dustman, apologizes to Rokesmith (it really is clear now that she loves him); when he leaves she collapses sobbing into Mrs Boffin's arms. She takes her leave, greatly moved in her impetuosity, and goes home.

righted i.e. what was wrong will be put right.
looking about the market for a good bid Certainly an uncompromising way of defining Bella's original mercenary intentions.
to book i.e. to account for what he has done.
a needy chap i.e. in need (of a job).
one down, t'other come on i.e. when we had finished with one, there was another to replace him.
Mew says the cat This extraordinary sequence is meant, it seems, to show that Mr Boffin has been reduced to behaving like an animal, but we know – or guess – it is all an act.
trumpery Worthlessness, nonsense.
a Duck . . . a Demon i.e. a good fellow . . . a very devil.

Chapter 16 The Feast of the Three Hobgoblins

Bella makes for her father's place of employment. They share Pa's simple tea and she is about to tell him what has happened when Rokesmith enters, takes her in his arms and calls her his 'courageous' girl. Bella confesses her love for him; Pa feels weak, and she sprinkles him with kisses and gives him a little milk to drink. When revived, Pa deduces the whole story and thoroughly approves. Eventually they leave to walk home; but after delays Rokesmith leaves them, and Bella and Pa are confronted by Mrs Wilfer, Lavvy and

George Sampson. There follows the news of Lavvy's courtship by George, and Mrs Wilfer and Lavvy have a brisk exchange of words. When it is all over and everyone has retired, Bella comes down again to tell her father of Rokesmith's prospects.

money-mills i.e. business, the stock-exchange, banks etc.
what o'clock it was i.e. what time it was.
turn-out i.e. dress.
Going i.e. fainting.
Gush i.e. outpouring (of news).
remarked i.e. noticed.
appliances of ceremony i.e. affectations.
like a frozen article The natural association of Russia with cold.
frail bark . . . seamanship Notice that even in this part of the plot the unifying sea image is used.
Saracen's Head . . . Dutch clock-work A combination of an inn sign and automatic movement.

Chapter 17 A Social Chorus

Following the seizure of the Lammles' furniture, the Veneerings are moved to give a dinner; and Mrs Lammle visits Twemlow – who, embarrassed and withdrawn, tells of the service rendered by Fledgeby. Mrs Lammle realizes, of course, precisely what Fledgeby has done for her, and she tells Twemlow that Riah is really the mask for Fledgeby's own unscrupulous machinations. Later, after Mrs Lammle has left, Twemlow goes to the Veneerings, where he finds a moody Eugene Wrayburn. Dickensian parody is very evident here, since the 'Fathers' of business are by analogy compared to the Fathers of the Church. There is much talk of the selling up of the Lammles, with pieces going for a song. Then young Blight appears, bringing Dolls to see Eugene, who prepares to leave.

twain The two of them.
inflammation i.e. acid indigestion, 'heartburn'.
beat up Invite, persuade.
will be found highly salutary A satirical glance at advertising.
Corinthian column A type of column, decorated with acanthus leaves, found in ancient Greek buildings; much copied since.
cabals i.e. conspiracies, cliques. (The word originated during the reign of Charles II, from the initials of the members of his 1672 Foreign Affairs Committee: Clifford, Arlington, Buckingham, Ashley and Lauderdale.)
table-d'hôte Here, a small hotel or boarding house, where there is a fixed menu at a set price, with no choice of food.
woolsack i.e. become Lord Chancellor.
Father of the Script-Church i.e. Those who control money. The tone is strongly satirical.
root and branch i.e. completely.
Navvies i.e. labourers, working men.
scouted i.e. scorned.
Gaming table . . . two establishments Implies gambling debts or supporting a wife and mistress.
off the box i.e. into the coach.
Glue Monge Rather apt rendering of 'blancmange'.

Book 4 A Turning

Chapter 1 Setting Traps

Wrayburn comes to Plashwater Weir Mill Lock, where Rogue Riderhood is the deputy lock-keeper, followed by a bargeman who turns out to be his shadow, Bradley Headstone. This time he is unseen by Eugene but, interestingly, he has dressed himself exactly like Rogue Riderhood. He is following Eugene, believing that the latter is going to see Lizzie. He gives Riderhood two sovereigns, but after he has gone Rogue decides to set a trap to find out whether or not Bradley is deliberately wearing the same clothes as himself. Later Bradley returns, sleeps briefly, then leaves to continue following Eugene. Two days later he returns, telling Rogue he has seen Eugene and Lizzie together. At one stage Bradley experiences – as he often does – a spurt of blood from the nose. Later he sleeps again, and Rogue discovers that he has adopted a red neckerchief similar to the one into which Rogue had (to test Bradley) changed.

wine of sentiment i.e. softer feelings.
Wagerbut A light boat used in races on which bets are placed.
the toll i.e. the money to be paid for using the lock.
teetotums Four-sided tops with letters on the sides to determine gain or loss of the spinner.
aggrawations Aggravations.
ekally Equally.
penny subscription i.e. a collection of a penny from each child.
Wat Tyler . . . City of London shield Wat Tyler was the leader of the Peasants' Revolt in 1381; the dagger shown on the shield was the one wrongly supposed to have killed him.
Lord Mayor Walworth i.e. he stabbed Wat Tyler, thinking the latter was going to kill the king.
The King Richard II.

Chapter 2 The Golden Dustman Rises a Little

Mr and Mrs Lammle are at breakfast with the Boffins, who are strangely silent during the witticisms of their guests. Mr Boffin in fact reprimands Sophronia because Mrs Boffin is upset; then he gives the Lammles one hundred pounds for services rendered. He asks them, too, if they were hopeful of replacing Rokesmith and Bella respectively, but tells them that he and they must go their separate ways. Just as they are leaving, Georgiana Podsnap bursts into the room. She is greatly upset that the Lammles are ruined and offers Sophronia three five pound notes she has saved, together with a necklace. She promises that if she is able, she will make some property over to them; she leaves. Mr Boffin has taken charge of the money and the jewellery so that they may be returned to Georgiana. Sophronia proves that she has a heart, but her husband is as hard as ever.

adage i.e. saying.
Court ... Lord Mrs Lammle is coyly playing at being in court. In a sense, she is on trial.
peroration Summing up.
reticule i.e. lady's netted bag.
chits i.e. young girls.
linked together by concealed handcuffs An appropriate image – they are linked by their own criminality.

Chapter 3 The Golden Dustman Sinks Again

Mr Boffin meets Venus, and they go to the Bower, where Wegg opens the door to them. Wegg is insolent, Boffin apparently cowed, and Wegg proceeds to put him in his place: among other things, he gets Sloppy sacked. After stating his intolerable terms, Wegg goes to Venus's with Boffin to examine the paper, and then escorts Boffin home. The latter is, apparently, completely humiliated.

excoriated Stripped of skin.
dash my wig You can be certain that . . .
to lump it i.e. put up with it.
the right-about i.e. at once.
atomspear Atmosphere. Wegg is becoming excited.
milk and watery i.e. easy-going.
the Roman Yoke Or, declining and falling, as he puts it on another occasion.
worrited i.e. worried.
Freemason i.e. member of a masonic lodge or society with its own rules, regulations and membership.
rostrum Platform for public speaking.
Gum-Tickler A neat spirit, here a tot of rum.
diwision i.e. division (of money).
an imaginary grindstone i.e. for rubbing Mr Boffin's nose, bringing him down (see chapter heading, 3,14,638).

Chapter 4 A Runaway Match

There is a conspiracy between Bella and R. Wilfer early one morning; soon after they set off for Greenwich to catch a steamboat. There they are met by Rokesmith, and walk to Greenwich Church; they are followed by an old pensioner with two wooden legs who is sympathetically portrayed, but is referred to only as Gruff and Glum. Bella and Rokesmith are married at the church, and the old pensioner attends. After the ceremony, Bella posts a letter she has previously written, telling Ma of her marriage and sending her love to Pa, thus exempting him from apparent connivance at the marriage. All three then proceed to a wedding breakfast at Mr and Mrs John Rokesmith's new cottage home at Blackheath. They go out for a ride and a walk, and again meet Gruff and Glum, who wishes Bella well. Bella, her husband and her father then dine together at the hotel in Greenwich to which Bella has previously taken Pa, who afterwards catches the steamboat home.

Two wooden legs ... Gruff and Glum This is odd to the point of being grotesque. But perhaps two wooden legs – as distinct from Wegg's one – makes the old man a complete and sympathetic character.
quids i.e. pieces of tobacco for chewing.
Rubric Direction for conduct of a service.
the queen's countenance on the letter i.e. a stamp.
Observatory ... Familiars of the Astronomer Royal The Royal Observatory was founded in 1675. The 'Familiars' would be the assistants there.
bring you to book i.e. to account.
warn't ... ji ... Wasn't ... joy ...
whatcheer A general colloquial greeting of the time. ('Wat'cher' still used by London's Cockneys.)
splice the main brace i.e. have a drink (to the happy couple).
Infant Bands of Hope A teetotal organization founded in 1855.
Papistical practice ... auricular Catholic practice ... told privately.
Archbishop of Greenwich i.e. the head waiter.
man on liking i.e. on trial.
excommunicated him Continuing the analogy, sacked him.

Chapter 5 Concerning the Mendicant's Bride

R. Wilfer returns home after the wedding and is shown Bella's letter to Ma, which, thanks to the efficiency of the Post Office of that time, has already been delivered. Mrs Wilfer gives a rich performance of being deeply hurt by Bella, and by the fact that she has married somebody with no money. Lavvy and George get caught up in a scene with Ma, but Lavvy makes it clear that she is her mother's own daughter. After they have all had their say, however, they decide they will receive Bella. R.W. dozes off – the best way to avoid the possibility of giving himself away. Bella appears with her husband a few weeks later, and sweeps all the family off their feet. On the way back, she and John discuss the fact of their having so little money. Their idyllic married life is described, and in particular Bella's contribution to it. Bella regrets very much that she has fallen out with Mrs Boffin. When Pa calls, Bella tends to treat him in a manner not dissimilar to Jenny Wren's with her 'child'. While John is seeing her father off one evening, Bella writes a long letter to Lizzie; when John returns, she reveals that she is going to have a baby.

Mendicant A beggar.
pew-opener Church attendant responsible for unlocking closed compartments of pews.
Viper i.e. betrayer.
between a sob and a bottle of soda water Again an instance of Dickens's imaginative use of words.
shallow sophistry The use of superficial and false arguments.
from her pedestal for his beguilement i.e. give up her act and make him happy.
China house i.e. trading with China, probably in silks, tea etc.
the Black Art i.e. witchcraft.
the Complete British Family Housewife A satirical glance at popular domestic books of the time, perhaps epitomised by Mrs Beeton.
Euclid The Alexandrian mathematician (c.300 BC), virtual founder of geometry.
grog Spirits and water.
curtain lecture i.e. wife's reproof to her husband.

Chapter 6 A Cry for Help

A description of a village Saturday evening after work has finished, and of a fair, open the chapter. Some distance away, Eugene Wrayburn walks beside the river and, unknown to him, the bargeman is watching. Lizzie meets Eugene and they talk; she tells him that she left London on his account; he in turn is impassioned and distressed. She begs Eugene to leave the neighbourhood, otherwise she will be forced to flee again. Both reveal their deepest thoughts and feelings, though more in suffering than tenderness. Against his will Eugene promises to try to leave the next day; he communes with himself when Lizzie has gone, though he is unable to resolve his dilemma. Shortly afterwards he collides with a man in the dark, and a little later is viciously attacked. Lizzie hears the noise and runs towards the spot. She sees Eugene in the water, hurriedly gets a boat out, passes a line around Eugene, pulls him in and gets him to the inn nearby. Surgeons come, but he is badly disfigured and barely alive.

Mrs Hubbard's dog According to the nursery rhyme, the dog was smoking a pipe after she had gone out to get him some tripe.
gingerbread i.e. a cake made with treacle and flavoured with ginger.
Barcelona Spanish port from which nuts would be exported.
Peep-show Small exhibition of pictures viewed through a lens.
osier-bed i.e. species of willow.
Napoleon Buonaparte at St Helena Eugene adopts the well known mock Napoleonic stance.
almost as he might have kissed the dead An ominous image almost foretelling his own death.
M.R.F. My respected father.
that old time i.e. when she rowed for her father.
Now, Merciful heaven ... Note the present tense which adds to the sense of urgency and excitement.

Chapter 7 Better to be Abel than Cain

Bradley Headstone returns to the lock. While he sleeps, news reaches Riderhood; afterwards the two men eat, and Bradley cuts himself, spilling blood on Riderhood. The latter tells Bradley that the news of Lizzie's finding the body has travelled down the river. When Bradley leaves, Rogue follows him, and sees him bathe and change his clothes. He continues to follow Bradley, who is not shaken by remorse but by the haunting fear that he has not done his deed well enough. The next day school re-opens; Bradley can think of little else than his attack on Eugene. Charley comes to see him, bringing the news that Eugene is dead. Bradley's ex-pupil denounces him for letting him (Charley) down. Charley is excessively sorry for himself; Bradley is abased. Meanwhile Riderhood recovers the telltale bundle of clothing from the river.

for'ard i.e. forward.
double honour An ambiguous – deliberately ambiguous – phrase, which implies deception.
You'll be for another forty on 'em A sleep, forty winks.
potation A draught.
elber i.e. elbow.
petted i.e. made a fuss of.
a Peck i.e. something to eat.

Chapter 8 A Few Grains of Pepper

Jenny is now living in seclusion, believing the worst of Riah. Her father is thinking of his betrayal of her and thus of Lizzie. Fledgeby comes to see Jenny, obviously trying to discover the whereabouts of Lizzie, blaming Riah and trying to bribe Jenny – she promises to visit him at his chambers in Albany at breakfast-time next day. Jenny ponders on the Riah/Fledgeby situation, but cannot make it out. When she gets to Albany she is prevented from going up to see Fledgeby by a lady, later revealed as Mrs Lammle. Jenny hears noises inside, goes in after Frederick Lammle has emerged, and finds that Fledgeby has been beaten and forced to take salt and snuff. When Jenny makes plasters of vinegar and brown paper for him, she adds a few grains of pepper.

backslidings i.e. relapsing into the old bad habits.
file Cunning old chap.
countermine Oppose.
tautology Saying the same thing twice over in different words.

However the cat jumps i.e. whichever way things go.
seemed to bowstring i.e. fire an arrow (at him).
Gargantuan Very large, enormous (from Gargantua, the giant created by the French writer Rabelais).
equipage i.e. carriage.
weales i.e. weals, bruises, marks.
vinegar and brown paper Perhaps a reminiscence of the nursery rhyme of Jack and Jill; Jack's head is mended with vinegar and brown paper.
Persian gown ... Persian cap Fledgeby varies his exotic garb – his previous attire was Turkish.
lay-figures Here, models; literally, manufactured models sometimes used by artists in place of living ones.

Chapter 9 Two Places Vacated

Jenny goes back and questions Riah. Being satisfied that Fledgeby and not Riah is behind Pubsey and Co. she begs his forgiveness and asks him to tell her the whole story. He does so, particularly recalling sitting in his garden on the housetop; he feels that he is blamed for many things because he is a Jew, but he has already written to Fledgeby, and is to be free of him the next day after he has served out his notice. Jenny now sees Fledgeby's motives for asking about Lizzie; Fledgeby sends Riah a 'good riddance' letter of dismissal, and the old man goes back home with Jenny. Meanwhile Dolls goes to Covent Garden, is set upon by urchins, obtains a drink by fraud and has a pail of muddy water thrown over him for his pains. He makes for the Temple; later he collapses and is picked up by the police. Jenny, accompanied by Riah, sees Dolls being carried in the street; he is dying, and Jenny is with him in the doctor's shop where he dies. She is distraught, but is greatly comforted by Riah; after her father's burial, she gets the idea of making a doll clergyman. Then Mortimer arrives, bringing with him the message that Eugene has requested that Jenny shall sit by him.

Capsicum i.e. chillies or hot peppers.
they ever got out of Egypt They were led out to the promised land by Moses.
hucksters i.e. pedlars and hawkers.
temporized i.e. reasoned.
no speculation in his See *Macbeth*, 3,4 again for an echo.
knock off i.e. finished.
the will for the deed i.e. the thought for the action.
Jack Robinson i.e. I am not who I am.

Chapter 10 The Dolls' Dressmaker Discovers a Word

Eugene, in a rare moment of understanding, reminds Jenny (who has come to stay at his bedside) of the children, the flowers and the birds that she once talked of, and also asks her to nurse him before he dies. He tells Mortimer too that he knows the person who has attacked him; but that he must never be brought to justice, since it is Lizzie's reputation that would suffer. Jenny understands his every move, and sympathetically reads his mind; when Eugene wakes again, Jenny tells Mortimer which word to say to him. It is the word 'Wife': Eugene wishes to make final reparation by marrying Lizzie.

what pavement is said to be made of good intentions The proverb is, 'The road to Hell is paved with good intentions': early examples of its use can be found in the writings of Dr Johnson and Sir Walter Scott.
sentient i.e. alive, having sense-perceptions.
ligature i.e. band or cord used to unite.
This frequent rising of a drowning man The image is again unifying: as we look back to Hexam (and across at Harmon), and forward to Bradley Headstone and Riderhood.
This is the right course of a true man, Eugene At his time of physical anguish, he finds the mental and emotional certainty so lacking hitherto – a frequent irony of 'real life'.

Chapter 11 Effect is Given to the Dolls' Dressmaker's Discovery

Bella is at her needlework, when Mortimer Lightwood comes to tell her that Lizzie wishes her to be present at her wedding. John arrives but refuses to see Lightwood, and Bella has to go off with the latter. The Milveys join them at the station in London though they are much delayed by Mrs Sprodgkin. Mrs Milvey sees Bradley there; he asks Milvey about Lizzie. Bradley thinks that Milvey may be going to conduct Eugene's funeral but Milvey tells him that she is going to be married. Later, an attendant tells Milvey that Bradley is having a fit. Milvey marries Eugene and Lizzie in a simple but moving ceremony.

anent Concerning, about.
smelling-bottle i.e. containing salts to revive a person who has fainted. In this case, providing timely relief.
Blue Beard of the secret chamber The wealthy castle owner who murdered his wives and was himself killed by the brothers of his last wife who had discovered the bodies of the others.
Clumsy-Boots i.e. your hands are like your feet.
marplot i.e. one who hinders something by being officious.
Amorites The powerful tribe of Canaan subdued by Joshua.
myrrh and frankincense ... locusts and wild honey Biblical references which underline Mrs Sprodgkin's obsession.
white one i.e. white lie, one that may be forgiven.
loadstone rock of Eternity i.e. all things are drawn towards their end.
utter helplessness of the wreck ... cast ashore Again, the unifying image.
mine Wealth.

Chapter 12 The Passing Shadow

Bella has her baby; but two or three months later sees that her husband is very uneasy. One day in London they unexpectedly meet Mortimer Lightwood, who recognizes John as Julius Handford; John returns home with Bella who, though worried, still has perfect faith in her husband. He then begins to tell her the story, but they are interrupted by Mr Inspector, who in the darkness has come into the room. He charges John with being in some way connected with the Harmon murder, but John retires with him for half an hour and when they return the Inspector is astonished. Later all three drive through the docks, go to the police station and then to the Porters, where the Inspector talks to Miss Abbey, and two men recognize John. Next day John tells Bella he has a new job, which means that they must move to a house in London provided with his new post: setting out to see the house the following day they arrive, to Bella's astonishment, at the Boffins.

frock-coat A long-skirted coat not cut away in front.
gravelled Puzzled, perplexed.
coughing and whistling satellites i.e. his subordinates.
a kind of criminal Pickford's i.e. the famous goods-carrying service, which dates back to the seventeenth century.
his order i.e. a fellow policeman.
writing-master i.e. making letters and words for copying.
gemplemorums i.e. gentlemen (or gentlefolk).

Chapter 13 Showing How The Golden Dustman Helped to Scatter Dust

The Boffins are delighted, for they are intent upon letting Bella know the true identity of John Rokesmith. Mrs Boffin tells how she came to recognize John one evening when he was sitting alone; the Boffins then explain to a confused Bella the plan of deception and what was really the testing of Bella. The Boffins reveal that they were even hidden at the marriage of John and Bella; all are delighted, and Bella determines to relate the rest of the story herself. Mr Boffin also tells how he has been deceiving Silas Wegg; and they all go off to inspect the *Harmons'* delightful new home.

Harkee i.e. listen.
picter i.e. the baby, 'pretty as a picture'.
the horses is off i.e. we've started, things are happening.
grislier old growler i.e. worse, more frightening old disagreeable man.
we were hard put to it i.e. we had to move quickly.
emissaries i.e. those sent on a journey or errand; here, a task.

Chapter 14 Checkmate to the Friendly Move

The last of the Mounds is removed; Silas is exhausted in the process; nothing of value is discovered. Wegg goes off to see Venus, who has had his place cleaned up by 'adorable woman', and Wegg is disgruntled by the sight; he arranges for the humiliation of Boffin next morning. When they are shown in, the Secretary flips off Wegg's hat, and Sloppy reveals that he has played the part of the foreman of the dust removal contractors who, by working day and night, have worn Wegg out. Venus discloses his part in the duping of Wegg; he also reveals that Mr Boffin and John have helped him with his courtship of Pleasant Riderhood. John Harmon then tells Wegg the story of the Dutch bottle; finally Wegg is thrown into the scavenger's cart by Sloppy.

black sheep ... sheared i.e. wicked man ... have his money taken.
fan-tail hat ... velveteen smalls Coal-heaver's hat or sou'wester; 'smalls' are knee-breeches.
dog-watches i.e. one of the two-hour watches (a nautical term).
setting up for lively i.e. making yourself out to be bright and cheerful.
kivering i.e. covering.
dudgeon Resentment.

its stock in trade i.e. the will found by Wegg.
flush of i.e. have many.
accoutred i.e. dressed.
dockyment i.e. document.
is quite another pair of shoes i.e. something completely different.
a scavenger's cart These toured the streets, picking up rubbish which they later sifted for sale. Wegg, in a sense, gets his just deserts.

Chapter 15 What Was Caught in the Traps That Were Set

Back to Bradley Headstone, his fits and his self-torture. One day, when he is teaching, Riderhood comes into the class-room: at his instigation, Bradley writes his own name on the blackboard; and in front of the class, Rogue mentions the clothing he has found (thrown into the river by Bradley); Bradley is blackmailed into going to the lock. Before doing so the following Saturday, Bradley leaves his watch with a note for Miss Peecher; by night-time he reaches Riderhood – who reveals how much he knows, and that he intends to drain Bradley of every penny he possesses. Rogue also reveals that when he called on Bradley he had previously visited the schoolmistress too. Bradley sits motionless throughout the night; early in the morning he goes for a walk, closely accompanied by Riderhood. On a second walk, Riderhood decides to change the lock-gates; and when both sets of gates are closed Bradley forces him – in a grip of iron – over the edge into the lock. Both are later found dead in the ooze behind one of the rotting gates.

that's in a churchyard The associations with death are obvious.
I'll pound it i.e. 'I'll bet on it'.
a-gin i.e. again.

slowly wiped his name out An ominous forecasting of his own death.

lecters Lectures.

I know to a figure I know exactly.

what bust from the blows i.e. what burst out from the blows (blood).

'spectable calling i.e. a respectable job.

a Saving's Bank book, or I'm a blue monkey i.e. (Miss Peecher) is as good as an investment, or I don't know who I am.

Bradley's iron ring i.e. his grip.

Chapter 16 Persons and Things in General

Mr and Mrs John Harmon exercise a benevolent patronage. Fledgeby is pursued and legally battered by Mortimer; and Twemlow is saved by John. Pa becomes Secretary; and Lavvy, George and Mrs Wilfer continue on their argumentative way. In fact, on a visit to Bella, Mrs Wilfer – in arctic mood – carries all before her. Sloppy visits Jenny Wren and, in another moving scene, offers (since he has been trained as a cabinet-maker) to make her four sets of nests for the dolls, and drawers for her sewing silks and scraps. Then Eugene – mending gradually – and Lizzie come to call on Bella and John. Eugene's marriage has the blessing of M.R.F.; Eugene has decided not to go to the Colonies; Mortimer decides to take another look at society.

trepanned Trapped, ensnared.

transatlantic dram ... eye-opener A strong mixed drink used as a morning pick-me-up: i.e. Young Blight was given new energy.

came to parley and asked for quarter i.e. decided to negotiate, and asked to be spared.

Corinthian column See note p.110.

brought up a young gazelle Apparently another echo of a ballad by Thomas Moore (1779–1852), the Irish poet and songwriter.

a pecuniary sense i.e. in a monetary sense.
take me up short i.e. disagree with my views.
ormolu Gilded bronze used in decoration.
gobbled ... gobbled i.e. went at it again and again.
the healthful music of my pulse For the quotation see *Hamlet*, 3,4.

Chapter 17 The Voice of Society

There is first of all a look into the future concerning the Veneerings (Mr Veneering's enforced resignation from Parliament is imminent). There is a satirical account of their inevitable dinner, which Mortimer attends. The guests – led by Lady Tippins and, of course, Podsnap – condemn the marriage of Eugene and Lizzie as being most unsuitable. However, Mortimer speaks out and, at last, Twemlow loses his mildness and supports the marriage in no uncertain terms.

Behoves (Also spelt 'behooves'); it is incumbent upon.
Books of the Insolvent Fates i.e. bankrupts.
overjobbed his jobberies i.e. been over-corrupt.
Chiltern Hundreds A sinecure office, which enables a member of Parliament to vacate his seat.
Neptune The sea god.
swain A lady's admirer or lover.
Robinson Crusoe ... the Island Robinson Crusoe is the famous castaway in the novel of that name by Daniel Defoe (1660–1731); it was published in 1719.
Juan Fernandez A mountainous island off the Chilean coast where the castaway Alexander Selkirk lived from 1704–9.
rattling sylph i.e. talkative beauty.
mésalliance i.e. badly matched pair.
moonshine i.e. visionary talk or ideas, unreal.
a bathing-woman and bolted i.e. a lady in charge of bathing huts, and ran off with her.
suffrages i.e. votes.

Questions

1 Compare and contrast Lizzie Hexam and Bella Harmon (née Wilfer).

2 Write an account of the part played in *Our Mutual Friend* by Silas Wegg.

3 What do you consider to be the main theme or themes of the novel? Refer to the text in support of your arguments.

4 Write an essay on the part played by *either* the river *or* the Mounds in *Our Mutual Friend.*

5 What do you learn of Dickens's views on education from this novel?

6 'Needlessly complex plot': how far would you defend Dickens from this accusation – as regards *Our Mutual Friend*?

7 Write an essay on the imagery used most frequently and tellingly in the novel.

8 A critic has suggested that the real title of the novel should have been *The Voice of Society*. In what ways do you think that a good title?

9 Write an account of the part played by *either* Jenny Wren or 'Fascination' Fledgeby in *Our Mutual Friend.*

10 How does Dickens create a particular atmosphere in this novel? In your answer, refer closely to the text.

11 Compare and contrast Rogue Riderhood and Bradley Headstone. In what ways do they differ?

12 Compare and contrast Eugene Wrayburn and John Harmon, bringing out their essential differences.

13 By close reference to two or three chapters, indicate the essential qualities of Podsnappery. What kind of comment is Dickens making through the presentation of this character?

14 Do you consider that the story of Betty Higden is 'overlaid with sentiment'? Give reasons for your answer.

15 'Money, money, money': in what ways is the plot of *Our Mutual Friend* built round this statement?

16 What elements of *Our Mutual Friend* do you find humorous, and why?

17 In what ways is the social background important to our understanding of *Our Mutual Friend*?

18 Write an appreciation of Dickens's use of symbol in this novel.

19 Indicate the nature of Dickens's use of his own voice in *Our Mutual Friend.* How far does it influence our own responses to the characters and their situations?

20 Write an essay on Dickens's use of pathos in *Our Mutual Friend.*

21. Show how Dickens conveys dramatic excitement by close reference to two or three incidents or scenes in this novel.

22 Write an account of the parts played by the Boffins in *Our Mutual Friend.*

23 With particular reference to any two or three characters, indicate Dickens's use of the grotesque in this novel.

24 Write an account of Dickens's presentation of marriage in *Our Mutual Friend.*

25 'Sombre and cynical': how far would you agree with this assessment of *Our Mutual Friend*?

26 Write an essay on the principles of unity in *Our Mutual Friend.*